# Table of Contents

# A Note From the Author

Reading is one of the most important life skills we'll ever acquire. However, to elementary students, the necessity of this ability down the road, and the fulfillment that can come from it, usually means little. Their lives are centered on instant gratification, and with the world as busy and data-driven as it is today, reading for pleasure has taken a back seat.

Just like anything else, to get better at something, one must practice. Readers are no different; they must practice, too—and competition for kids' time from television, video games, computers, the Internet, and music has made the job of "hooking" them on reading more difficult and ever more important. In this environment, when a child does discover that reading really *can* be fun and is not just a mundane means to an end, when a child *does* begin to develop lifelong reading skills and the urge to read more and more, it is all the more rewarding to see.

Encouraging readers is a passion of mine that became a career choice. As a media specialist, I want kids to want to read. I want them to enjoy reading, to see the importance of it. If rewards and incentives are what it takes to get kids started reading, then so be it; I have developed and employed reading incentives with great success throughout my career, and they have only served to enhance my students' reading experience.

Thirteen of my favorite library incentive parties are included in this book, and it is my hope that teachers and media specialists will incorporate some or all of them into their reading programs with wild success. Be sure to read the introduction on page 5 for some helpful hints that may be useful to you as you get started. Good luck, have fun, and happy reading!

—Dr. Carol Thompson

# LIBRARY
# INCENTIVE
# PARTIES

BY DR. CAROL THOMPSON

**UpstartBooks**

Janesville, Wisconsin

*This book is dedicated to Kimm Smith,*
*who taught me to ask, "What is best for the kids?"*
*and who helped me to understand that learning can be fun.*
*Thanks, buddy!*

Published by UpstartBooks
401 South Wright Road
Janesville, Wisconsin 53547
**1-800-448-4887**

Copyright © 2010 by Dr. Carol Thompson
Cover design: Debra Neu

The paper used in this publication meets the minimum requirements of American National Standard for Information Science — Permanence of Paper for Printed Library Material. ANSI/NISO Z39.48-1992.

# Introduction

## What Is a Library Incentive Party?

A library incentive party is the culmination of a themed reading unit or program designed to get kids motivated to read. This book is a collection of ideas, or incentives, for themed units and culminating parties. Each incentive chapter includes a summary of the incentive's theme, party, and reading record (a motivational recordkeeping tool that helps students to track their progress, and helps the media specialist track who receives party invitations); bulletin board ideas; and food and decoration recommendations.

Additionally, every chapter features suggested reading and related Web sites, useful reference questions, and a detailed list of theme-related activities that you and your students can do in advance of the party. Many of these incentive activity lists include webquests, which I have found to be a great tool to use for independent enrichment work. Webquests get students learning about the Internet and practicing keyboarding skills, all while gaining insight into a particular topic. They are also highly motivating and fun! Sometimes I require certain students to complete a webquest to satisfy a requirement of a theme's reading record.

Getting kids to read a variety of literature is the ultimate goal of a library incentive party program. If you, the media specialist, can assist in teaching curricula along the way, that is just one of many bonuses that benefits the students—and their teachers! Here are some time-tested suggestions to help:

- **Allow Time for Planning & Set Time Limits**

  A well-executed project is a well-planned project. Brainstorm the incentive's theme—be sure to think about any and all materials, activities, and food that may be included. Collect your ideas in a folder. Just because you don't use every item this year doesn't mean you won't two years down the road. Don't try to do every activity in your overall plan. Pick and choose. Don't spend too long on any one theme.

- **Remember the Point of the Party**

  Although there exists an enormous amount of material that could be used during your program, the idea is to introduce kids to an assortment of genres and library skills, and to instill a love of reading. Never forget that these are the primary roles of the media specialist. When it comes time to throw the party, go all out whenever possible, because a great time will get kids truly celebrating reading—and get them excited for your next party!

- **Be Flexible**

  Children's reading abilities and interests are different, even though they may be in the same grade level. While preparing your overall goal for student reading, take teacher suggestions into account. The idea is for the student goal to be achievable, yet effort-worthy. Always remember initiative and effort in the overall scheme of things. While you do not want to make your incentives too difficult to achieve, you do want to challenge students to earn their reward and feel pride in their accomplishment.

- **Be Organized**

  After you decide which activities will be used, make copies of what you need and put the rest of the folder away. Know when your classes are coming and have materials ready ahead of time.

- **Take Notes**

  As your activities progress, take notes of what works, what doesn't, and what kids liked or didn't like. Also be sure to note whom you borrowed decorating objects from, and who donated what for your parties. Another helpful piece of advice is to write down how many students were served at the party and how much of each food item was needed. Because you may not do this party in consecutive years, it is easy to forget— write it down!

- **Take Pictures/Make Memories**

  There is no better way to remember your incentive parties than by taking lots of pictures. I always make double prints and share with partygoers. It also serves as a reminder of "how things looked" for the next time you conduct a similar party.

# A Doggone Good Reading Party

## Incentive Summary

What better (and cuter) way to motivate kids to read than with the world's most popular pet: the lovable puppy! This particular incentive is fun, easy, and covers a broad range of curricular objectives. It is also easily adapted to multiple grade levels.

I do lots of joint planning with my clerk and other teachers to help narrow down which activities we do in the media center. In our resource file we keep many other activities that teachers can use at their discretion. While in the media center, students are exposed to "Bow WOW!" activities that cover multi-curricular objectives. There are activities that can be completed at school and at home. To be invited to the "Doggone Party" at the end of the month, students must earn the privilege. For example, kindergartners may have to read 20 books at home and have appropriate documentation to show for it. One way that this can be done is to give them a spotted reading record Dalmatian bookmark to keep up with their books. Every book that they read earns a dot sticker on the Dalmatian (or they can color in the spots themselves). When students have accumulated twenty "spots," they are invited to the party. (For reproducible bookmark template, see page 11.)

Older students may have to accumulate ten points in the accelerated reader program on their reading level using books related to pets, or specifically, dogs. (Sometimes, I require that older students read nonfic-

tion exclusively.) The media specialist should keep in mind to always make the goal attainable. The object is to have students motivated enough to read, but able to successfully reach the goal too. During the month, while students are working independently on their reading goals, we hold Doggone/Bow WOW! activities in the media center. (See below for suggested activities.)

At the end of the month, we celebrate those students who have reached their goal by having a "Doggone Good Reading Party." After assembling the guest list, each student receives an invitation to the party. Some years we have focused on one special dog like Clifford, or just dogs in general.

## Food and Decoration Ideas

For our Doggone parties, decorations include dog-related party supplies from the local party center. Party food includes a doggone good cake in the shape of a puppy's paw, puppy chow (Chex or Trail Mix), and juice boxes; and, of course, all of the food is served in dog bowls purchased from the dollar store. The classes that participated throughout the month made dog ears (something that might also be done with help from the art teacher; see page 13 for pattern), and we all wore them at our party too.

We also take a group picture as well as individual pictures for the school scrapbook. Each student is given a certificate to commemorate this special event (for reproducible sample, see page 12). One year, instead of having our traditional party, we planned a real dog event. The best part was that it served two purposes being that it was fun and educational. We had the sheriff's office bring in the K–9 unit to our school. They celebrated with us as well. The dog handler discussed the training process to the students, the dog's physiology, and the effects of drug use. He also demonstrated how the drug task force used the K–9 unit.

## Bulletin Board/Display

Here is a sample of a Doggone It, READ! bulletin board. When we add a display, we also title it "Doggone It, READ!" and arrange related books and materials such as stuffed animals, dog treats, etc., around it. (For book suggestions, see suggested reading at the end of this chapter.)

## Cafeteria Menu

Advertise your incentive program in newsletters, newspapers, and the school Web site. When the whole school participates in an event, students know it must be important. Even the lunchroom can spread a positive atmosphere about the theme. Here are some suggestions:

- Hot DOGS
- Dog Biscuits
- Clifford's Red Jello
- Wishbone's Chicken
- Dalmatian Dessert (vanilla pudding with crumbled Oreo cookies)
- Peanut "Pet-ter" and Jelly Sandwiches
- Paw Print cookies

## Suggested Incentive Activities

- Students make dog ears from the reproducible pattern on page 13. They wear their ears during storytime and also during the party.
- Read biographies of famous Hollywood or rescue dogs.
- Conduct a doggone webquest! See page 14 for reproducible instruction sheet.
- Have the local sheriff's office arrange a visit from the K–9 unit
- Coordinate a pet day to coincide with this themed unit.
- Using the online catalog, have students find and categorize books about dogs/ pets/animals.
- Hide "You found me!" dog bones (see page 15 for reproducible sample) in several books and resources around the library. Have students form groups, and provide each group with a set of call numbers or other hints (see page 16 for reproducible sample), and send them on a dog bone treasure hunt!
- Brainstorm famous real/fictitious dogs (ex. Clifford vs. Balto).
- Research responsible pet ownership. Get started with Web sites such as www.aspca. org/pet-care and www.hsus.org/pets.
- Younger students can play games and explore on www.scholastic.com/clifford or www.pbs.org/arthur. (There is a special page for his lovable pet puppy, Pal.)

- Older students can do mini research papers on a specific breed of dog.

- Create separate graphs to monitor favorite pets by class

- Have a representative from the animal shelter visit. Read about and discuss possible duties prior to the visit.

- Have the principal or other teacher walk around the school and "dognap" kids who are found reading. Have principal send such readers with a certificate (see page 17 for reproducible sample) to the media center for a special prize.

- Jokes are a good way to promote what is happening in the media center. It gets kids involved and curious. Morning announcements are an opportune time to reach out to the whole student population. Here are some doggone good ones that can be read by a student:

  - What is a dog's favorite city? *(New Yorkie!)*

  - What kind of dog loves to take a bath? *(A shampoodle!)*

  - What kind of dog do vampires prefer? *(A bloodhound!)*

  - What do you call a happy Lassie? *(A jolly collie!)*

  - Why aren't dogs good dancers? *(They have two left feet!)*

  - Where should you never take a dog? *(To the flea market!)*

  - How does a dog stop the DVD player? *(He presses the paws button!)*

  - Why did the Dalmatian go to the eye doctor? *(She kept seeing spots!)*

# Reference Questions

Have a question of the day on the school intercom, or have a grade-appropriate question displayed during library time and teach students how to find answers. Students can research answers in various ways and turn them in to the media center for prize drawings at the party. Make sure that students document where they found the answer (see page 18 for a special "Research Hound" reproducible sample). Use your imagination—this is a great way to portray the importance of the library reference section. Some suggested questions include:

- What was the name of the famous Siberian husky that led his team 650 miles from Nenana to Nome carrying Diptheria serum? *(Balto)*

- What was Snoopy's sister's name? *(Belle)*

- The farmer had a dog and his name was... *(Bingo)*

- What was the name of the dog in Alyssa Capucilli's famous series of books? *(Biscuit)*

- This constellation is named after the two dogs owned by Orion. *(Canis Major)*

- What was the name of the hound dog in Disney's "Fox and the Hound"? *(Copper)*

- What was the name of Hagrid's dog in the Harry Potter series? *(Fluffy)*

- Who owns the famous dog, Pluto? *(Mickey Mouse)*

- What is the name of the University of Georgia's mascot? What kind of dog is it? *(Uga/Bulldog)*

- What book did dogs Little Ann and Old Dan come from? *(Where the Red Fern Grows)*

- In *The Grinch Who Stole Christmas*, what was the Grinch's dog's name? *(Max)*

## Suggested Reading

Books should always be available around the bulletin board and/or display for student motivation and reference. Students should also be encouraged to venture outside the school library for further material. Here is a good start for this theme:

*   *Arthur's New Puppy* by Marc Brown. LB Kids, 2005.

*   *Bathtime for Biscuit* by Alyssa Capucilli. HarperCollins, 1999.

*   *Because of Winn-Dixie* by Kate DiCamillo. Candlewick Press, 2009.

*   Clifford books by Norman Bridwell, from Cartwheel.

*   *Dog of Discovery: A Newfoundland's Adventures with Lewis and Clark* by Laurence Pringle. Boyds Mills Press, 2004.

*   *Fred Stays with Me!* by Nancy Coffelt. Little, Brown Young Readers, 2007.

*   *Irish Red* by Jim Kjelgaard. Yearling, 1984.

*   *Just Me and My Puppy* by Mercer Mayer. Random House, 1998.

*   *Little Polar Bear and the Husky Pup* by Hans De Beer. North-South Books, 2004.

*   *Love That Dog* by Sharon Creech. HarperCollins, 2001.

*   *My New Boy* by Joan Phillips. Random House, 1986.

*   *Police Dogs* by Frances Ruffin and Wilma Melville. Bearport Publishing, 2005.

*   *Shiloh* by Phyllis Reynolds Naylor. Atheneum, 1991.

*   *Stone Fox* by John Reynolds Gardiner. HarperCollins, 1992.

*   *The Tenth Good Thing about Barney* by Judith Viorst. Aladdin, 1987.

*   *Where the Red Fern Grows* by Wilson Rawls. Delacorte, 1996.

*   *Where is Spot?* by Eric Hill. Putnam, 2005.

*   Wishbone series by Brad Strickland and Caroline Leavitt, from Big Red Chair Books.

## Related Web Sites

*   ***American Society for the Protection of Cruelty to Animals***, www.aspca.org/pet-care

*   ***Arthur Web site on PBS***, www.pbs.org/arthur

*   ***Clifford Web site***, www.scholastic.com/clifford

*   ***Humane Society of the United States***, www.hsus.org/pets

# Dalmation Bookmark

Student Reading Record: Color in each dog's spots for your required reading.

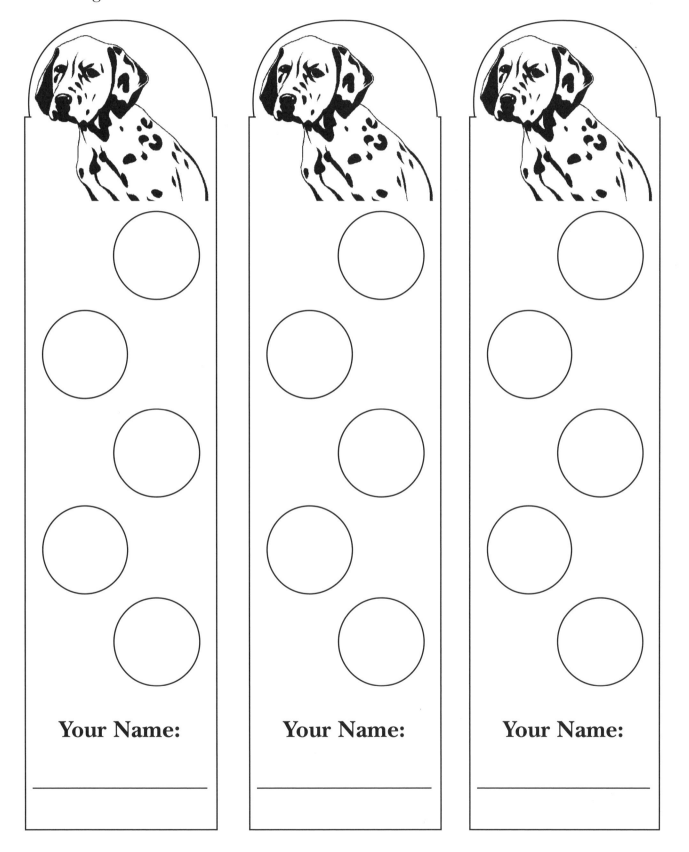

**Your Name:**

**Your Name:**

**Your Name:**

# No Bones About It!

_____

is a doggone good reader!

_____                    _____

Media Specialist Signature                              Date

# No Bones About It!

_____

is a doggone good reader!

_____                    _____

Media Specialist Signature                              Date

# Dog Ear Pattern

**Directions:** Using tape and two strips of brown or yellow paper 1" thick, create a band to go around each child's head (resting above the ears). Have children cut out two dog ears from the pattern below, color both sides, and tape or staple to the band.

# Dogs in Depth Webquest

Visit the Web site www.dogsindepth.com. Set your timer for 15 minutes.
When time is up, choose five of your favorite dog breeds and complete the chart.

| Dog Breed & Origination | Average Height and Weight | Physical Traits | Personality or Temperament | Cut and Paste Picture of Dog | Name Your New Pet |
|---|---|---|---|---|---|
| | | | | | |
| | | | | | |
| | | | | | |
| | | | | | |
| | | | | | |

You found me!
GREAT JOB!

You found me!
GREAT JOB!

You found me!
GREAT JOB!

Reproduce pattern and write call number and title on bone. Pass out to groups for team competition. The group that finds all of their dog bones first wins.

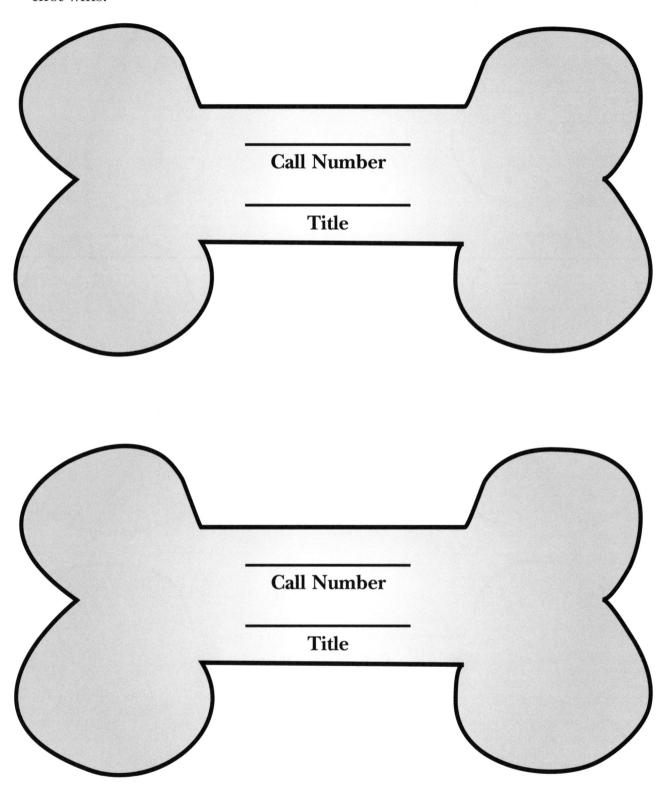

## I've been Dog-Napped!

’cause I was reading

(good for 30 minutes in the media center)

## I've been Dog-Napped!

’cause I was reading

(good for 30 minutes in the media center)

# I'm a research HOUND!

The question: _____

The answer: _____

Where I found this answer: _____

_____

_____

My name: _____

My teacher: _____

# I'm a research HOUND!

The question: _____

The answer: _____

Where I found this answer: _____

_____

_____

My name: _____

My teacher: _____

# Hit a Home Run with Reading!

## Incentive Summary

This is a great October (World Series month) or springtime incentive. Using the theme of America's pastime, baseball, students are encouraged to hit a home run and celebrate their favorite teams and players while learning about the history of America's best-loved sport.

Readers keep up with their stats on a baseball field reading record sheet (see page 23 for reproducible sample). The baseball diamond can be changed to accommodate different grade levels or individual needs. Readers advance on their reading records' bases by achieving their reading goals, and they must score a home run in order to earn an invitation to this particular incentive party, which at our school has included a school-hosted all-American hotdog and apple pie cookout, and tickets to the community minor league or local baseball team (I always try to plan a "School Night," when everyone can be at the game together). Another option is to give tickets to the local high school baseball game, or, to have your home-run-hitting readers play an actual game of whiffle ball against the teachers.

Whatever you decide, celebrating reading will be a hit! So join the World Series or Spring Training anticipation with this reading incentive and encourage your students to step up to the plate. This month-long unit will prove to be a fun learning experience for everyone!

## Food and Decoration Ideas

For this incentive, we plan an old-fashioned, all-American hotdog and apple pie party. The menu includes hotdogs, chips, sodas, juice, and apple pie, either homemade, or from McDonalds. Decorations might include patriotic or baseball-themed flags, napkins, tablecloths, plates, and bunting. www.orientaltrading.com is one of many online sources for such decorations; your local party store may carry them, too.

## Bulletin Board/Display

Here is a sample of a "Hit a Home Run with Reading!" bulletin board. Get creative! Baseball bats and baseballs can create great letters. It also looks good to use old book covers on this bulletin board for a 3-D effect.

## Cafeteria Menu

Advertise your incentive program in newsletters, newspapers, and the school Web site. When the whole school participates in an event, students know it must be important. Even the lunchroom can spread a positive atmosphere about the theme. Here are some suggestions:

- Baseball Burgers
- 1st Base Franks
- 2nd Base Spaghetti
- Short Stop Shortbread Cookies
- Catcher Corn Dogs
- Pitcher Pizza
- Fastball Fries
- Double-play Pudding
- Curve Ball Casserole
- Home Run Ham
- Knuckle Ball Nuggets

## Suggested Incentive Activities

- Visit mlb.com/mlb/kids/mail_call.jsp on the Internet and have students write a letter to a favorite player, manager, or coach. Teach and/or review proper form for a friendly letter.

- Act out *Casey at Bat* theatrically.

- Have a favorite team dress-up day where students wear their baseball/softball uniforms. (For a real treat, include hats—if they are normally against your dress code, kids will love it!)

- Have students complete the Louisville Slugger Factory Museum webquest on page 24.

- Have the high school baseball or softball team players or coaches come and read to classes during storytime.

- Have a mock baseball game using library questions (correct answers earn a base hit for the offensive team).

- Locate baseball-related books. Categorize them after printing a shelf list.

Have students play in teams. Using the call numbers of the books, see which team locates the most in a 10-minute period.

- In groups, write a new poem similar to *Casey at Bat* (upper grades), but title it *Casey with His Book.*

- Watch the video "How a Baseball Bat is Made" on www.youtube.com or www.break.com.

- Have a debate about the best baseball player ever (students must defend their opinions with facts based on research in almanacs or other reference books).

- Have the school nurse or local college coach discuss steroids (upper grades).

- Younger grades can learn the song "Take Me Out to the Ballgame" and act it out. The music teacher can also help with this activity.

- Rewrite "Take Me Out to the Ballgame" to a new version "Take Me Out to the Library." Perform it over closed circuit for advertisement.

- Discuss reference sources to find the best option for researching Lou Gehrig's disease. After reading his biography, discuss the disease.

- Brainstorm baseball-related words. Using the dictionary, copy the part of speech and definition on a bat for display.

- Label all the major league teams and stadiums on a U.S. map.

- Jokes are a good way to promote what is happening in the media center. It gets kids involved and curious. Morning announcements are an opportune time to reach out to the whole student population. Here are a few that can be read by a student:

- Why does it get hot after a baseball game? *(Because all the fans leave.)*

- What takes longer, running from 1st base to 2nd base or from 2nd base to 3rd base? *(2nd base to 3rd base, because you have a shortstop.)*

- Why did the baseball player take his bat to the library? *(Because his teacher told him to hit the books.)*

- Why did Cinderella get kicked off the baseball team? *(Because she ran away from the ball.)*

- What do you get when you cross a tree with a baseball player? *(Babe Root)*

- Why did the baseball player get arrested during the middle of the game? *(Because he got caught stealing 2nd base!)*

- How are pancakes and a baseball game similar? *(They both depend on the batter.)*

- What has 18 legs and catches flies? *(A baseball team)*

- Which baseball team also takes care of sick animals? *(The New York VETS)*

- Why didn't the dog play baseball? *(Because he was a BOXER.)*

## Reference Questions

Have a question of the day on the school intercom, or have a grade-appropriate question displayed during library time and teach students how to find answers. Students can research answers in various ways and turn them in to the media center for prize drawings at the party. Make sure that students document where they found the answer. Use your imagination—this is a great way to portray the importance of the library reference section. Some suggested questions include:

- In baseball, what does the term "south-paw" mean? *(A left-handed pitcher)*

- Where is Wrigley Field located? *(Chicago)*

- What is the term used to define a player who has played for one year or less? *(rookie)*

- What pitcher holds the all-time record for most games won and also has a prestigious award named after him? *(Cy Young)*

- Who was nicknamed the Iron Man, and why? *(Cal Ripken, because he never missed a game in 2,632 games.)*

- In 2001, who was the highest paid Latino baseball player? *(Alex Rodriguez)*

- Where is the National Baseball Hall of Fame located? *(Cooperstown, New York)*

- Who were the two inductees to the 2007 Hall of Fame? *(Cal Ripken and Tony Gwynn)*

## Suggested Reading

Books should always be available around the display for motivation and reference reasons. Students should also be encouraged to venture outside the school library for further material. Here is a good start!

- *Ballpark: the Story of America's Baseball Fields* by Lynn Curlee. Aladdin, 2008.

- *Baseball's Brilliant Managers* (The Sports Heroes Library) by Nathan Aaseng. Lerner Publishing Group, 1982.

- *Casey at Bat* by Ernest Thayer. Handprint Books, 2000.

- *Casey Back at Bat* by Dan Gutman. HarperCollins, 2007.

- *Diamond Life: Baseball Sights, Sounds, and Swings* by Charles Smith, Jr. Orchard Books, 2004.

- *Grand-Slam Riddles* by Joanne E. Bernstein and Paul Cohen. Albert Whitman, 1988.

- *H is for Home Run: A Baseball Alphabet* by Brad Herzog. Sleeping Bear Press, 2004.

- *Hank Aaron* by George Sullivan. Putnam, 1975.

- *Home Run: The Story of Babe Ruth* by Robert Burleigh. Silver Whistle, 1998.

- *Jackie Robinson* (Trophy Chapter Book) by Kenneth Rudeen. Harper Trophy, 1996.

- *Just a Baseball Game* by Mercer Mayer and Gina Mayer. Golden Books, 2003.

- *Lou Gehrig: The Luckiest Man* by David Adler. Voyager Books, 2001.

- *Louisville Slugger: the Making of a Baseball Bat* by Jan Arnow. Knopf Books for Young Readers, 1984.

- *Mama Played Baseball* by David Adler. Gulliver Books, 2003.

- *Mighty Jackie: The Strike-Out Queen* by Marissa Moss. Simon & Schuster/Paul Wiseman Books, 2004.

- *Mudball* (Tavares Baseball) by Matt Tavares. Candlewick Press, 2005.

- *Out of the Ballpark* by Alex Rodriguez. HarperCollins, 2007.

- *Play Ball, Amelia Bedelia* by Peggy Paris. HarperCollins, 1996.

- *Players in Pigtails* by Shana Corey and Rebecca Gibbon. Reed Business, 2003.

- *Strange But True Baseball Stories* by Furman Bisher. Random House, 1966.

- *The Babe & I* by David Adler. Tandem Library, 2004.

- *The Bat Boy and His Violin* (Aladdin Picture Books) by Gavin Curtis. Aladdin, 2001.

- *The Magic School Bus Plays Ball: A Book About Forces* by Joanna Cole. Scholastic, 1998.

## Related Web Sites

- Baseball Hall of Fame. www.baseballhall offame.org

- Louisville Slugger Museum. www.slug germuseum.org

- Major League Baseball fan mail addresses. mlb.com/mlb/kids/mail_call.jsp

- Major League Baseball Kids' Dugout www.mlb.com

- PBS: Baseball History. www.pbs.org/ kenburns/baseball

- Sports Illustrated for Kids. www.sikids. com

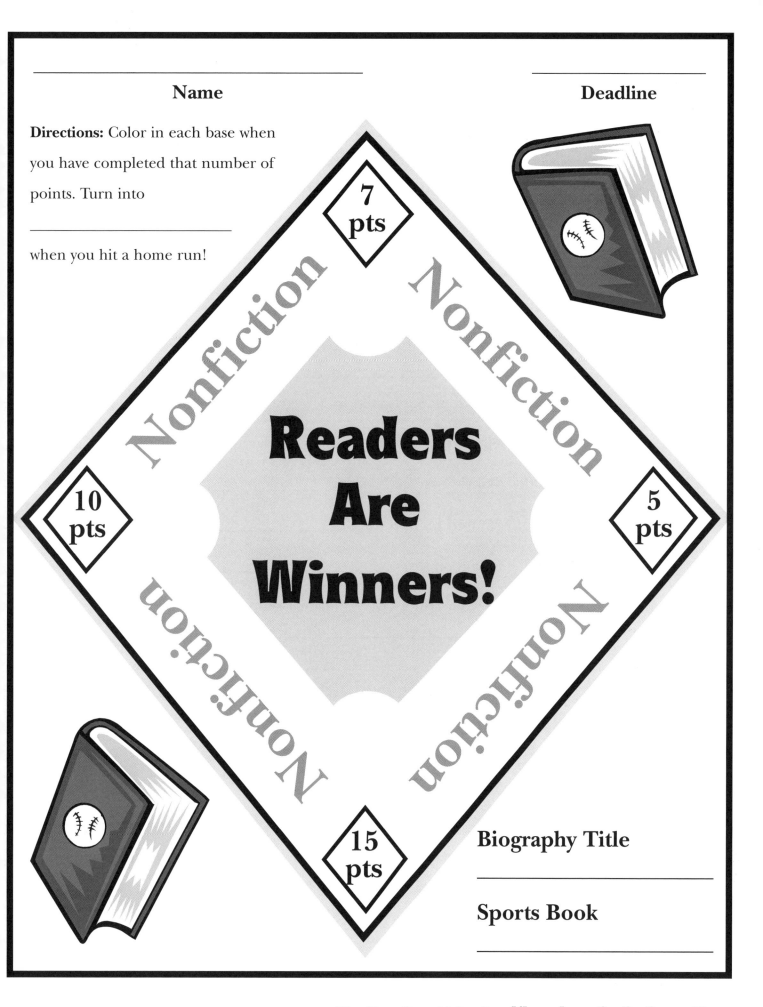

**Name**

**Deadline**

**Directions:** Color in each base when you have completed that number of points. Turn into _____ when you hit a home run!

7 pts

Nonfiction

Nonfiction

10 pts

**Readers Are Winners!**

5 pts

Nonfiction

Nonfiction

15 pts

**Biography Title**

**Sports Book**

# Louisville Slugger Museum & Factory

**www.sluggermuseum.org**

1. How much does the world's biggest bat weigh? _____

2. Who made the first Louisville Slugger baseball bat ever? _____

3. How much does it cost for a ten year old to visit? _____

4. In what year was the 125th anniversary of the first Louisville Slugger baseball bat?
   _____

5. What type of wood is used to make Louisville Slugger Baseball Bats? _____

6. How many Louisville Slugger baseball bats are made each year? _____

7. How much does the "Baby's First Bat" cost? _____

8. What is the current Featured Exhibit titled? _____

9. How long does the exhibit run for? _____

10. What are the two awards that Hillerich & Bradsby Company give out? Explain each. _____
    _____

11. Who won the first Silver Bat award? _____

12. What player has won the most Silver Bat awards thus far? How many?
    _____

13. What number is always present on a Louisville Slugger baseball bat? _____

14. On a separate sheet of paper, write a newspaper article inviting people to visit the Louisville Slugger Museum & Factory. Remember to add a catchy title!

15. On a separate sheet of paper, draw a picture of how the outside of the factory looks.

# S'more Reading, Please!

## Incentive Summary

This camping theme is a hit in the fall. What better way to spend a crisp autumn evening than with a book, a campfire, and of course, s'mores? This incentive is sure to entice boys and girls alike. At our school, we base activities on themes of nature, environmental awareness, camping, and sweet, delicious s'mores. Families are encouraged to partake in the activities and the culminating bonfire celebration: a school-hosted Family Reading Campout under the stars. Roasting hot dogs and marshmallows are only half the fun—students who meet their reading goals will earn special privileges at the event!

Have students track their reading accomplishments on the s'more-building progress tracker (see page 29 for reproducible sample). Encourage parental cooperation with this theme by requiring students to read at home at least 20 minutes a night. Also, require students to read one nonfiction book that is theme related. As students progress, have parents or guardians sign their reading record, and send incentive party invitations to those students who complete their reading record.

There are several options for the Family Reading Campout. One option is to have a family movie night under the stars with an inflatable movie screen. These can be purchased or rented from party stores. Another idea is to have a professional storyteller perform around the bonfire, where families will be listening and making s'mores! Students who met their reading goals should have special privileges, such as reserved seats around the campfire, being the storyteller's aides, etc. They should also be recognized at the event with a certificate (see page 30 for reproducible sample).

## Food and Decoration Ideas

- Clusters of fun camping gear lit up with flashlights (tents, backpacks, tarps, etc.)
- Battery-powered candles
- Piles of warm blankets
- Hot dogs and potatoes for roasting
- Hot chocolate

## Bulletin Board/Display

Here is a sample of our S'more Reading, Please! bulletin board. Get creative! Cotton balls make great bulletin board marshmallows. For a display, consider creating a homemade paper campfire, around which you place stuffed animals reading books.

## Cafeteria Menu

Advertise your incentive program in newsletters, newspapers, and the school Web site. When the whole school participates in an event, students know it must be important. Even the lunchroom can spread a positive atmosphere about the theme. Here are some suggestions:

- Camping Casserole
- Pigs in the Sleeping Bag
- Trail Mix
- Little "Smokies" (cocktail weenies)
- Tent Tacos
- Evergreen Salad
- Fishing Poles (pretzel sticks with red licorice and a gummy worm on the end)

## Suggested Incentive Activities

- Have students complete the S'more Fun on the Web activity sheet on page 31.

- Invite a representative from a state park to come talk about camping safety and wildlife.

- Go on a nature walk and collect fallen leaves. Using reference aids in the media center, identify the leaves and make a collage.

- Read biographies about Smokey the Bear.

- Using the Web site www.jpkid.com or www.nps.gov, choose one state where there is a JellyStone campground or a national park. Use different methods to route your trip from your hometown to the campground or park (atlas, Web-based map, etc.).

- Using the reproducible map of the United States on page 32, label all the national parks in the appropriate places with the tent symbol.

- Using www.weatherchannel.com, have students check and record the weather at the state parks in their state for the weekend.

- Have students form groups to come up with a National Park motto. Start by brainstorming different words (stewardship, conservation, preservation, integrity, magnificence, etc.).

- As a class, categorize a camping packing list (food, equipment, clothing, etc.).

- Invite the Boy Scouts/Girl Scouts to come and explain how they earn their patches, or interview student members.

- Have students work in groups to come up with a scary campfire story.

- Using the online catalog, find and categorize books about camping, nature, and/or chocolate (s'mores).

- Make a "Thinking Word Bank" using the following criteria: the five senses and a campfire circle (e.g., What do I smell around a campfire? What is that snapping, crackling noise? What is that I smell? Smoldering wood?).

- Have students rewrite the recipe for s'mores and hypothesize about the reaction (e.g., gummi worms, saltines, and popcorn). Publish papers in a classroom campfire newspaper.

- Have the music teacher teach the Smokey the Bear song found at www.smokeybear.com.

- Have students create a campaign poster on the prevention of forest fires.

- Have younger students make binoculars out of empty toilet paper tubes and "look for books." Ask them to record their findings in a log of books they would like to read.

- Have older students run in group relay races in P.E. to see how quickly their group can pitch a pup tent. This is a great collaboration activity for following directions.

- Jokes are a good way to promote what is happening in the media center. It gets kids involved and curious. Morning announcements are an opportune time to reach out to the whole student population. Here are a few that can be read by a student:

  - What's green, round, and goes camping? (A boy sprout!)

  - What side of the fish has the most scales? (The outside)

  - Why are baseball players handy at a campout? (They pitch the tent!)

## Reference Questions

Have a question of the day on the school intercom, or have a grade-appropriate question displayed during library time and teach students how to find answers. Students can research answers in various ways and turn them in to the media center for prize drawings at the party. Make sure that students document where they found the answer. Use your imagination—this is a great way to portray the importance of the library reference section. Some suggested questions include:

- Which president was responsible for establishing the National Park System? (Theodore Roosevelt)

- In 2003, what Disney animated movie profiled Smokey the Bear as a character? (Bambi)

- What does the abbreviation RV stand for in camping terms? (Recreational Vehicle)

- Name three ways you can help to prevent forest fires. (Answers will vary.)

- Name two movies that are camping related. (Answers will vary.)

- What is the Boy Scout's motto? (Be prepared)

## Suggested Reading

- *Bailey School Kids #50: The Abominable Snowman Doesn't Roast Marshmallows* (Bailey School Kids) by Marcia Thornton and Debbie Dadey. Scholastic Paperbacks, 2005.

- *Camping Catastrophe* (Ready, Freddy!) by Abby Klein. Blue Sky Press, 2008.

- *Cooking on a Stick: Campfire Recipes for Kids* (Activities for Kids) by Linda White. Gibbs Smith Publishers, 2000.

- *Cowboy Camp* by Tammi Sauer. Sterling Publishing, 2005.

- *Froggy Goes to Camp* (Froggy) by Jonathan London. Viking Juvenile, 2008.

- *The Graves Family Goes Camping* by Patricia Polacco. Puffin, 2008.

- *Little Camp of Horrors* (Mostly Ghostly) by R.L. Stine. Delacorte Books for Young Readers, 2005.

- *Marshmallow Clouds* by Dr. Leslie Parrott. Zonderkidz, 2005.

- *Marshmallow Kisses* by Linda Crotta Brennan. Houghton Mifflin, 2007.

- *Matthew and Tall Rabbit Go Camping* by Susan Meyer. Down East Books, 2008.

- *The Night Before Summer Camp* (Reading Railroad Books) by Natasha Wing. Grosset & Dunlap, 2007.

- *S is for S'mores: A Camping Alphabet* (Sleeping Bear Alphabets) by Helen Foster James. Sleeping Bear Press, 2007.

- *Toasting Marshmallows: Camping Poems* by Kristine O'Connell George. Clarion Books, 2001.

## Related Web Sites

- *Camping equipment*, www.campamerica.com

- *Enchanted Learning*, www.enchantedlearning.com (search for lesson plans on camping)

- *Jellystone Park for Kids*, www.jpkid.com

- *National Park Service*, www.nps.gov

- *Smokey the Bear*, www.smokeybear.com

- *Weather Channel*, www.weatherchannel.com

# Build Your S'mores

|  | Monday | Tuesday | Wednesday | Thursday | Friday |
|---|---|---|---|---|---|
| **1.** (S'mores) | Title of Book | Title of Book | Title of Book | Title of Book | Title of Book |
| **2.** (S'mores) | Title of Book | Title of Book | Title of Book | Title of Book | Title of Book |
| **3.** (S'mores) | Title of Book | Title of Book | Title of Book | Title of Book | Title of Book |

# Reading Achievement!

_____
Student's Name

S'more Reading, Please!

Picture
Of
Student

# Reading Achievement!

_____
Student's Name

S'more Reading, Please!

Picture
Of
Student

# S'more Fun on the Web

**Visit the Smokey the Bear profile at
www.smokeybear.com/kids to complete these sentences.**

Smokey is a _____ bear. He can weigh up to _____ pounds. But when he was born,

he only weighed about _____ pounds, which is about the size of a _____ .

Smokey's favorite clothes include a _____, _____, and _____ .

He can also usually be seen standing upright with a _____ in his hand.

Smokey's favorite saying is " _____ _____ _____ _____ _____ ."

Smokey's favorite foods include _____ .

Smokey's relatives' favorite winter activity is heavy sleep. This is also called _____ .

They eat a year's worth of food in _____

months so they have a layer of fat that keeps

them fed during the winter sleep.

Be careful the next time you are camping and

making s'mores, and remember to

always put out your _____ !

— — — — — — — — — — — — — —

Answers (cut off at line above if you do not wish to
distribute answers to students): Black; 800; 1.5; big
loaf of bread; personalized ranger hat, blue jeans,
and belt; shovel; "Only you can prevent wildfires.";
hibernation; 6–8 months; campfire

# Let's Go Camping!

**Directions:** Using the National Park Service Web site (www.nps.gov) or the JellyStone Web site (www.jpkid.com), locate and label a campground in at least 20 states. Bonus points for more states. Make sure you name the state, the the city or town where the campground is located, and label it with a tent, as indicated by the legend..

**Legend:**

Campground

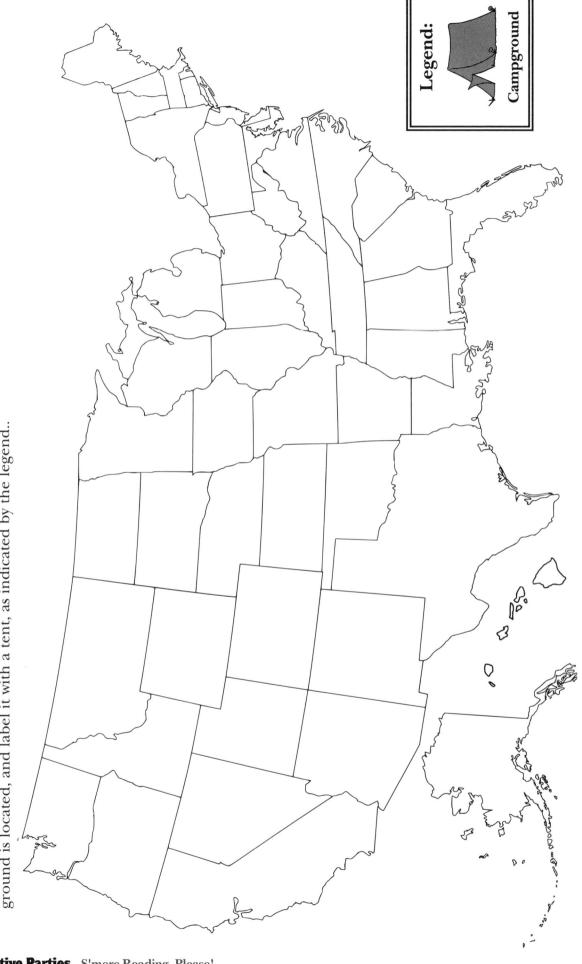

# Got Game?
# Got Books?

## Incentive Summary

It is hard to compete with the allure of video games, so this library incentive party was developed to use the games themselves as part of the motivation. Whatever it takes to get kids to read is worth the effort!

Building on the popularity of video games, students are encouraged to read about not only the history and technology of the actual machines, but also any fictional books with video gaming as the subject. Before they receive invitations to the culminating Got Game? Got Books? Library Video Game Tournament Party, students are asked to complete a video game reading record puzzle, which provides them with a constant visual (and gaming) reminder to read. It also makes it easier for the media specialist when it comes time to send out the invitations.

To create the reading record, reproduce the puzzle on page 36 for each student according to directions there. Cut the pieces of card stock according to the puzzle lines (get volunteers to help you, and be sure to keep the puzzles separate!). When a student has collected all the puzzle pieces for his assigned bag, have him assemble the puzzle. When the puzzle is assembled, the student receives an invitation to the Got Game? Got Books? Library Video Game Tournament Party!

## Food and Decoration Ideas

For our Got Game? Got Books? Library Video Game Tournament Party, we have included:

- Pac Man Popsicles found at our local supermarket

- Medallions for the top winners

- Certificates for all participants (see page 37 for reproducible sample)

- Video game cake (for decorating ideas, visit www.coolest-birthday-cakes.com/birthday_cake_ideas_for_kids.html or similar sites)

For the video game tournament component to this party, we have had guests compete head-to-head in an all-out Xbox tournament on a 30-foot inflatable screen in the school library or gym, depending on participation. We purchased this screen, but they can also be rented. In the long run, it saves money to just go ahead and buy one.

As always, the goal is to get kids extremely excited about reading and achieving a reading goal, and the inflatable screen has that effect. However, if a large screen is a stretch, an inspiring party can still be had with several gaming systems set up to individual monitors! (Ask for donations of systems from families or local businesses, or see if any of your students' families might be willing to let you borrow their system for the day.)

No matter what you decide, be sure the competition is friendly. Depending on the number of players, brackets may need to be created, and different times for parties established. Students might choose to play on teams or play individually.

## Bulletin Board/Display

Here is a sample of a Got Game? Got Books? bulletin board.

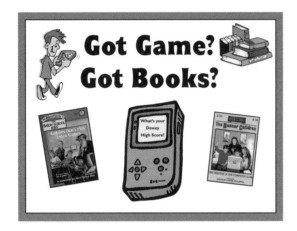

## Cafeteria Menu

Advertise your incentive program in newsletters, newspapers, and the school Web site. When the whole school participates in an event, students know it must be important. Even the lunchroom can spread a positive atmosphere about the theme. Here are some suggestions:

- Pac Man Pizza
- Nintendo Nachos
- Playstation Pasta
- Joystick Jello
- Pokemon Pudding
- Donkey Kong Doughnuts
- Mario's Macaroni
- Game "Cubed" steak
- Dream Cast Dessert

## Suggested Incentive Activities

- Work in groups to come up with a new video game with a "Library Maze" theme.

- Have students research the history of the video game. Use chart paper to make detailed time lines.

- Explore electricity. Work with science teachers to make a circuit breaker.

- Categorize video games into themes.

- Write a persuasion paper for or against allowing video games in school. (Younger students should write a persuasion paragraph.) Use those papers to have a debate.

- Vote for the student body's favorite video company and video game.

- Graph results and publicize them either on intercom, newsletter, or Web site. (Younger students should use tally marks.)

- Have students create a campaign and advertisement for an imagined video game.

- Students have a Video Game Swap Meet or Used Sale (profit buys books).

- Conduct a video game webquest, such as the one on page 38.

- Encourage art. Have students design a character for a Library Monster Game.

- Jokes are a good way to promote what is happening in the media center. It gets kids involved and curious. Morning announcements are an opportune time to reach out to the whole student population. Here are a few that can be read by a student:

- Why are cats good at video games? (*Because they have nine lives!*)

- What kind of video game would you most likely find at a campsite? (*Nin-TENT-O*)

- What did the video game player say when he went down the slide? (*"Wiiiiii!"*)

## Reference Questions

Have a question of the day on the school intercom, or have a grade-appropriate question displayed during library time and teach students how to find answers. Students can research answers in various ways and turn them in to the media center for prize drawings at the party. Make sure that students document where they found the answer. Use your imagination—this is a great way to portray the importance of the library reference section. Some suggested questions include:

- Using an almanac find the best selling video game of 2006. (*Madden NFL 07*)

- What was the top selling game of 1997? (*Nintendo 64 Mario Kart*)

- Electronic games or video games are controlled by a tiny computer called a _____. (*microprocessor*)

- Besides having to do with video games, what is another definition for the term "arcade"? (*A series of arches supported by columns or piers, either free standing or attached to a wall to form a gallery*)

## Suggested Reading

Books should always be available around the bulletin board and/or display for student motivation and reference. Students should also be encouraged to venture outside the school library for further material.

Here is a good start for this theme:

- *The Boys Upstairs* by C.S. Richard. iUniverse, Incorporated, 2006.

- *The Case of the Video Game Smugglers* (Can You Solve the Mystery) by M. Masters. Abdo, 1992.

- *Attack of the Video Villains* (The Hardy Boys #106) by Franklin Dixon. Aladdin, 1991.

- *Boy from Nowhere* by Antonio Olson. Liberty Bell Production, 1999.

- *Goblins Don't Play Video Games* (The Adventures of the Bailey School Kids, #37) by Debbie Dadey and Marcie Jones. Scholastic Paperbacks, 1999.

- *Lucky Leaf* by Kevin O'Malley. Walker & Co., 2007.

- *Mercer Mayer's LC+ The Critter Kids: Showdown at the Arcade* (A Golden Book School Time Reader) by Eric Farber. Golden Books, 1994.

- *The Ultimate History of Video Games from Pong to Pokemon: The Story Behind the Craze that Touched Our Lives and Changed The World* by Steven Kent. Three Rivers Press, 2001.

- *Video Rivals* (First Novel Series) by Sonia Sarfati. Formac Publishers, 1995.

## Related Web Sites

- *Birthday cake ideas*, www.coolest-birthday-cakes.com/birthday_cake_ideas_for_kids.html

- *How Stuff Works* (search "How video game systems work"), www.howstuffworks.com

- *Online games*, www.yahooligans.com

**Teacher Directions:** Each student receives a puzzle (printed on heavy card stock) already cut out. As they put the puzzle together, they must complete the required reading. After the puzzle is finished, the student may tape it together and turn it in to the media specialist.

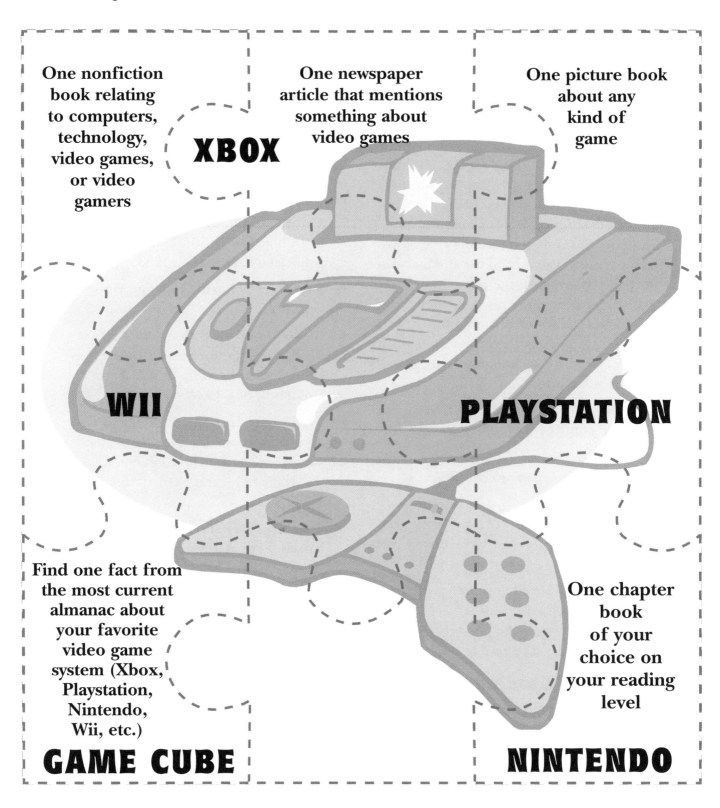

One nonfiction book relating to computers, technology, video games, or video gamers

**XBOX**

One newspaper article that mentions something about video games

One picture book about any kind of game

**WII**

**PLAYSTATION**

Find one fact from the most current almanac about your favorite video game system (Xbox, Playstation, Nintendo, Wii, etc.)

**GAME CUBE**

One chapter book of your choice on your reading level

**NINTENDO**

# You've Got GAME!

High Score Awarded to:

_____

because you completed all
reading requirements.

_____          _____
Date                Media Specialist

---

# You've Got GAME!

High Score Awarded to:

_____

because you completed all
reading requirements.

_____          _____
Date                Media Specialist

# Video Game Webquest

Directions: Explore the Web sites below and use the information you find to complete the webquest below.

➤ **Gamer:** _____

1. Review the timeline at www.time.com/time/covers/1101050523/console_timeline. In what year was the first video game console that worked on a standard television invented? _____

2. Review the timeline at www.time.com/time/covers/1101050523/console_timeline. In 1995, Sony Playstation games cost less than other consoles. Why?

   _____

   _____

   _____

3. Review the timeline at www.time.com/time/covers/1101050523/console_timeline. What major handheld game console was released in 1989?

   _____

4. Name one game title for each major brand of video game. If you get stuck, visit the brand's Web site.

   Nintendo DS (www.nintendo.com):  _____

   Xbox 360 (www.xbox.com):  _____

   Playstation 3 (www.us.playstation.com/PS3): _____

   Wii (www.nintendo.com):  _____

5. Using your knowledge of video games and the Web sites above, come up with as many categories as you can for types of video games. For example, SPORTS could be one category. _____

   _____

   _____

   _____

   _____

# Video Game Webquest

## Answer Key

1. Review the timeline at www.time.com/time/covers/1101050523/console_timeline. In what year was the first video game console that worked on a standard television invented? **1967**

2. Review the timeline at www.time.com/time/covers/1101050523/console_timeline. In 1995, Sony Playstation games cost less than other consoles. Why?

   **Playstation games used CD-ROM technology, which was not as expensive as game cartridge technology.**

3. Review the timeline at www.time.com/time/covers/1101050523/console_timeline. What major handheld game console was released in 1989?

   **Game Boy**

4. Name one game title for each major brand of video game. If you get stuck, visit the brand's Web site.

   Nintendo DS (www.nintendo.com):   **Anwers will vary.**

   Xbox 360 (www.xbox.com):   **Anwers will vary.**

   Playstation 3 (www.us.playstation.com/PS3):   **Anwers will vary.**

   Wii (www.nintendo.com):   **Anwers will vary.**

5. Using your knowledge of video games and the Web sites above, come up with as many categories as you can for types of video games. For example, SPORTS could be one category.   **Anwers will vary.**

# American Girls Read!
## An American Girl Tea Party

## Incentive Summary

Many young readers enjoy series books, and the American Girl series often ranks among the series options. Not surprisingly, this month-long incentive is especially popular with girls at our school. After reading from the American Girl series (Pleasant Company Publications) and completing the American Girl webquest and other activities (see below for ideas), students are invited to attend a very special culminating tea party in the library to celebrate all the readers' participation. The holidays are a great time to do this incentive because a "Holiday Tea" is a fun way to make readers feel special, and promote etiquette—both in and out of the library!

Once invitations are sent out (see page 43 for reproducible sample), students participate in an authentic tea party complete with finger sandwiches (cut into small triangles; crustless), shortbread cookies, and warm tea. I like to make this an intimate personal tea so we divide it up by grade levels. We set a formal place setting at a well-decorated table with candles, linen napkins, fresh flowers, and fine china. We also put place cards for each special guest (see page 44 for reproducible sample). Guests are invited to bring their favorite American Girl or other doll to the tea. I always make sure to take pictures and include them on participants' reading certificates (see page 45 for reproducible sample). Activities and games are optional.

## Food and Decoration Ideas

The Pleasant Company offers event kits mainly for bookstores to purchase. Some larger bookstores will donate their older kits to school libraries once they are done. They can be purchased directly through the company's Web site as well. If this incentive is done during the month of December, the decorations can be hand made by choosing one particular era. Party supply stores also offer some American Girl party theme paper supplies.

## Bulletin Board/Display

Here is a sample of an "American Girls Read!" bulletin board. Get creative! Using a pattern with a hand mirror and digital pictures inserted into the middle makes this display very attractive. (Another option is to purchase authentic American Girl party decorations for your bulletin board from www.americangirl.com.) A tablecloth makes a great background.

## Cafeteria Menu

Advertise your incentive program in newsletters, newspapers, and the school Web site. When the whole school participates in an event, students know it must be important. Even the lunchroom can spread a positive atmosphere about the theme. Here are some suggestions:

- Addy's apples
- Felicity's French fries
- Josefina's gelatin
- Kit's kringles
- Molly's mashed potatoes
- Samantha's spaghetti

## Suggested Incentive Activities

- Have students complete an American Girl webquest (see reproducible pages 46–48 for two options).

- Invite girls from the local high school to come and read to classes. Try to get volunteers with a wide range of interests (athletes, musicians, science/math/language/volunteer club participants, artists, thespians, etc.)

- Have a weekly dress-up day (one week could be historical American Girls, another could be modern American Girls, etc.). Make sure to take pictures for the paper!

- Coordinate with each grade level's social studies teacher and spotlight the American Girl and an excerpt from her book that coincides with the social studies curriculum.

- Students can shadow successful businesswomen of the community—ask friends, mothers, grandmothers, sisters, and aunts to volunteer!

- Host career talks from successful businesswomen.

- Read biographies of real women who have made a difference.

- Create a new American Girl with a name, time setting, and description.

- Make an alphabet book listing possible new names for the next American Girl.

- Make a Venn diagram comparing different characters.

- Coordinate with math teachers to show a real-world application of math skills using the American Girl online store and the American Girl Web site, and compose a wish list from the online store (store.americangirl.com/agshop/static/home.jsf).

- Talk about why there might be so many different authors for the American Girls series and locate their different books using the online catalog.

- Write a letter to a favorite American Girl and tell them about how life is different or the same today.

- Make a time capsule containing items typical of an American girl today.

- Define and discuss historical fiction. Give examples using American Girls as well as other book characters.

- There are lots of American Girl craft books. Choose one or two crafts to do over a class period (some may take more than one). After-school book club time is an especially great time to do these. Parent volunteers come in handy with these types of projects.

## Reference Questions

Have a question of the day on the school intercom, or have a grade-appropriate question displayed during library time and teach students how to find answers. Students can research answers in various ways and turn them in to the media center for prize drawings at the party. Make sure that students document where they found the answer. Use your imagination—this is a great way to portray the importance of the library reference section. Some suggested questions include:

- What real American "girl" is known for founding the Girl Scouts? (*Juliette Gordon Lowe*)

- Who designed the Vietnam Veterans Memorial in Washington DC? (*Maya Lin*)

- Who was the first woman to swim across the English Channel, breaking the men's record? (*Gertrude Ederle*)

- Who was the first African American woman elected to public office? (*Shirley Chisholm*)

- Who wrote a series of autobiographical tales of her childhood as a pioneer girl? (*Laura Ingalls Wilder*)

You could also ask American Girl-specific questions, such as:

- Which American Girl wears glasses? (*Molly*)

- Which American Girl is mostly associated with the Civil War era? (*Addy*)

- Which American Girl would most likely use the word "pueblo"? (*Josefina*)

## Suggested Reading

Books should always be available around the bulletin board and/or display for student motivation and reference. Students should also be encouraged to venture outside the school library for further material. Here is a good start for this theme:

- American Girl character series by various authors. (Addy, Felicity, Elizabeth, Josefina, Julie, Ivy, Kaya, Kirsten, Kit, Ruthie, Molly, Emily, Rebecca, Samantha, Nellie) Pleasant Company Publications.

- American Girl Cooking Studios Series. (four titles.) Pleasant Company Publications. American Girl Mini Mysteries series. (12 titles.) Pleasant Company Publications.

- American Girl Short Story Collection. (eight titles.) Pleasant Company Publications.

## Related Web Sites

- American Girl. www.americangirl.com

- American Girl Publishing. www.americangirlpublishing.com

# You are cordially invited to a Reading Tea Party!

**RSVP to**

_____

**\*\*Bring your favorite doll\*\***

# You are cordially invited to a Reading Tea Party!

**RSVP to**

_____

**\*\*Bring your favorite doll\*\***

Reserved for American Girl

Name

Reserved for American Girl

Name

Reserved for American Girl

Name

Reserved for American Girl

Name

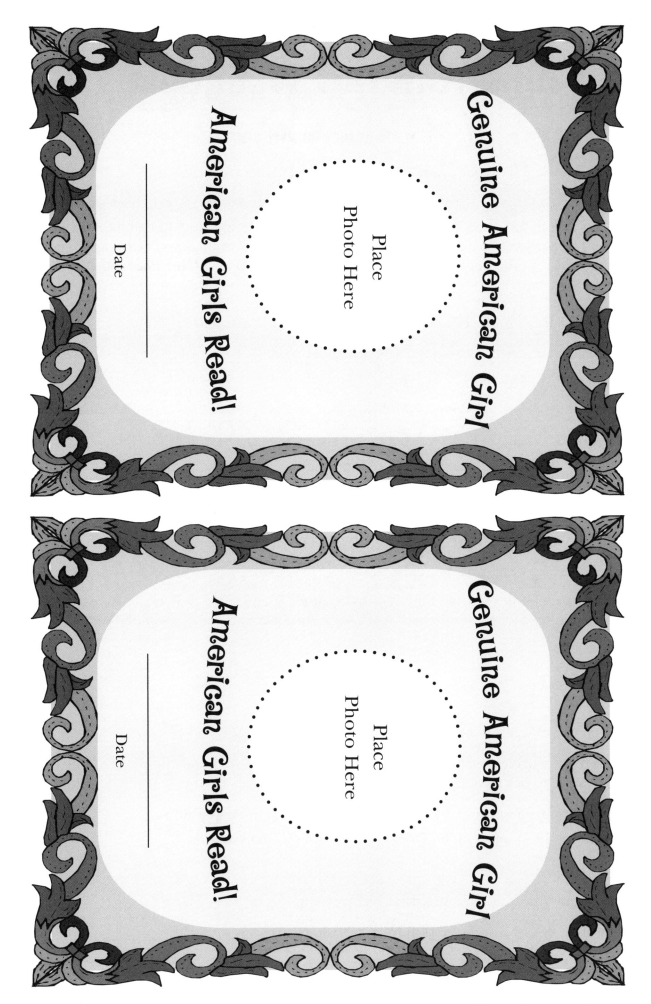

**Genuine American Girl**

American Girls Read!

Place Photo Here

Date

**Genuine American Girl**

American Girls Read!

Place Photo Here

Date

# American Girl Webquest 1

## www.americangirl.com

Name: _____

Teacher: _____

**Directions:** Go to the American Girl Web site and have fun exploring. Remember, if you get stuck, you can always use the "back" button to return to the last page you were on or click on "American Girl" in the upper left corner to go to the Homepage. Remember our Internet rules. After you have explored, answer the following questions:

1. List the years with which these historical characters are associated:

   Julie: _____          Addy: _____

   Kaya: _____          Kit: _____

   Felicity: _____          Molly: _____

   Josefina: _____

2. What kind of animal is Licorice?_____ Coconut? _____

3. Play one of the Magazine Activities then write its name here: _____

4. Go to the magazine's quiz section and complete a quiz. Which quiz did you select?

   _____

5. Go to Take A Doll's Journey and select a location. Spend some time exploring your location and learning more about it. Then, write a summary of what you learned.

   Location: _____

   Summary: _____

   _____

6. Which year was Marisol the Girl of the Year? _____

7. Search for activities related to A Smart Girl's Guide to Money and choose one "make your own" piece to design and print. Attach it to this worksheet.

8. Go to "About American Girl" and find the answers to these questions:

   When was the company founded? _____ Who was the founder? _____

   What happened in 1998? _____

   How many visits does the American Girl Web site receive each year? _____

   How long does a visit to the Doll Hospital usually take? _____

# American Girl Web Quest 2

## www.americangirl.com

Name: _____

**Directions:** Go to the Web site above. Have fun exploring. Remember if you get stuck you can always use the back button to return. Remember the Internet rules your teacher gave you. After you have explored, complete the quest below.

1. Where are the seven locations of the American Girl stores? _____
   _____

2. List the top games in the Fun for Girls! section. Choose one to play and tell about it.
   _____
   _____

3. Visit the Shop section. How much does the Kaya doll with the accompanying book cost? _____

4. If you won $224.00 to spend at the store or boutique, list what you would buy and the items' prices. You must have only $5.00 or less when you leave.
   _____
   _____
   _____

5. Visit the E-Card Central page and email an e-card to someone special. Staple a hard copy to this webquest.

6. Which year was Chrissa the Girl of the Year? _____

7. Search for upcoming special events at the American Girl stores. Select one event that you would like to attend, and make a flyer to advertise your choice. Staple a hard copy of your flyer to this webquest.

# American Girl Webquest

## Webquest 1 Answer Key

1. Julie: __1974__        Addy: __1864__

   Kaya: __1764__        Kit: __1934__

   Felicity: __1774__        Molly: __1944__

   Josefina: __1774__

2. Licorice is a cat and Coconut is a dog.

3. Answers will vary.

4. Answers will vary.

5. Answers will vary. Options are: Hawaii, Belize, London, Paris, Tanzania, Singapore, and Australia.

6. 2005

7. See student's attachment to this sheet.

8. 1986; Pleasant T. Rowland; Mattel purchased American Girl; 52 million; about two weeks

## Webquest 2 Answer Key

1. Atlanta, Boston, Chicago, Dallas, Los Angeles, Minneapolis, New York

2. Answers will vary.

3. $95.00 - $100.00

4. Answers will vary.

5. See student's attachment to this sheet.

6. 2009

7. See student's attachment to this sheet.

# Reading Pays!

## Incentive Summary

Money is one of the world's greatest motivating factors, even for kids. What better way than money to motivate students to read? This month-long "Reading Pays" incentive is fun anytime, but works especially well in February because of President's Day. After students have "invested" their time in reading, they "earn" money and get paid "dividends" by receiving invitations to a party.

For students to earn an invitation to the Reading Pays Party, they must earn $9.99 (which corresponds to the highest Dewey classification) by reading. The amount of money can be changed to accommodate different grade levels or individual needs. Students are given a piggy bank reading record (see page 53 for reproducible sample) and earn money by reading appropriate books. For example, they can earn a penny by reading a magazine article. They can earn up to $5.00 for reading a biography about one of the presidents on any currency. Play money or clip-art money copied on construction paper can be used to staple to the piggy bank once they earn it; alternatively, a coin reproducible is available on page 54. The media specialist should keep the money and "pay out" only when the student can document their reading.

When the student earns $9.99 or more, they are invited to the Reading Pays Party. There are several options for this party depending on your funds and time. For an inexpensive celebration, coordinate your book fair at the time of this unit. Give out "book fair bucks" for prizes; students can spend their bucks on books. Another idea is to rent a wind blowing money machine from a party supply store. Use play money and let students use their money to buy other pre-selected items. The movie "Richie Rich" is always a favorite way to culminate the money month. Whatever your budget, the payout will be rewarding!

## Food and Decoration Ideas

- Green punch

- Million dollar sheet cake. This is an inexpensive and fun treat. Search free clip art and photo Web sites for an image of a bill you like, download it, and place a picture of yourself or another media specialist in the middle of the currency. Take the digital file you've created to a bakery that does airbrushing.

- Individually wrapped coin chocolates (found at party supply stores)

- A reproducible Reading Pays certificate can be found on page 55.

## Bulletin Board/Display

Here is a sample of a "Reading Pays" bulletin board. Get creative! We had fun using monopoly money and book covers.

## Cafeteria Menu

Advertise your incentive program in newsletters, newspapers, and the school Web site. When the whole school participates in an event, students know it must be important. Even the lunchroom can spread a positive atmosphere about the theme. Here are some suggestions:

- Penny Pasta
- Money Honey biscuits
- "Quarter" lb. cheeseburgers
- "Po-Boy" Sandwiches
- "Rich" chocolate brownies
- Million dollar Meat Loaf
- Silver dollar Steaks
- Paycheck Pizza
- Nickel Nuggets
- Dime Doughnuts
- "Broke" biscuits
- Banker's Bologna Sandwiches
- U.S. Mint mints

## Suggested Incentive Activities

- Invite a banker to come in during story-time and share a little about his or her career.
- Direct students to conduct a card catalog search on books about money and sort them into categories such as fiction, non-fiction, and reference.
- Take a field trip to a local bank or credit union. Make a Venn Diagram comparing and contrasting the difference between a bank and a credit union.
- In groups, have students come up with a poem or song entitled, "Reading Pays!"
- With a partner, have students think about the question, "If a book is worth its number of characters in gold, I'd read _____." Teams try to come up with a body of work (a story, magazine, reference book, etc.) with the most characters. Start with a hint, like *Snow White and the Seven Dwarfs.*
- Have students conduct the U.S. Mint webquest on page 56.
- Get students to bring in the oldest penny they can find, and make a time line using the penny collection. Have students use an almanac to find one important event that happened for each year represented. Use long chart paper to illustrate. Display in hallway.
- Have students campaign and elect one new person to put on U.S. currency. Direct them to work in teams to draw new pictures of coins and bills. Teams must justify why they chose their fictional or real person. They can use biographies or reference section. In my school, past examples have included Rambo, Martin Luther King, Babe Ruth, and even Santa Claus!
- Have a two-week coin drive to raise funds for books. Allow students to do the ordering after money is collected. What books will they choose for their library?
- Research Fort Knox. Use a Smart Board to take a virtual trip.

- Using an almanac, have students locate the top grossing book sales for the year. Let them take the data to math class to discover the mean, median, mode, and other information based on current objectives.

- Watch a video on how the U.S. Treasury makes and circulates money.

- Jokes are a good way to promote what is happening in the media center. It gets kids involved and curious. Morning announcements are an opportune time to reach out to the whole student population. Here are a few that can be read by a student:

  – What do you get when you cross a woman on a broom with a millionaire? *(A very witch person!)*

  – Why is money called dough? *(Because we all knead it!)*

  – What is the fastest way of doubling your money? *(Fold it in half.)*

  – What do you call a man with a lot of money? *(Bill)*

  – What money do you use under the sea? *(Sand dollars)*

  – How much money does a skunk have? *(One scent)*

  – Where do penguins keep their money? *(In a snow bank)*

  – Where do frogs borrow money? *(From the river bank)*

  – Why did the farmer bury his money? *(He thought it would make his soil richer.)*

  – What did the penny say to the $100 bill? *(You're worth a lot of money, but you make no cents!)*

  – Why did the boy swallow three dollars? *(Because it was his lunch money.)*

## Reference Questions

Have a question of the day on the school intercom, or have a grade-appropriate question displayed during library time and teach students how to find answers. Students can research answers in various ways and turn them in to the media center for prize drawings at the party. Make sure that students document where they found the answer. Use your imagination—this is a great way to portray the importance of the library reference section. Some suggested questions include:

- Whose face is on the $1.00 bill? *(George Washington)*

- Whose face is on the $2.00 bill? *(Thomas Jefferson)*

- Whose face is on the $5.00 bill? *(Abraham Lincoln)*

- Whose face is on the $10.00 bill? *(Alexander Hamilton)*

- Whose face is on the $20.00 bill? *(Andrew Jackson)*

- Whose face is on the $50.00 bill? *(Ulysses S. Grant)*

- Whose face is on the $10.00 bill? *(Benjamin Franklin)*

- Whose face is on the penny? *(Abraham Lincoln)*

- Whose face is on the nickel? *(Thomas Jefferson)*

- Whose face is on the dime? *(Franklin Roosevelt)*

- Whose face is on the quarter? *(George Washington)*

- Whose face is on the half dollar? *(John F. Kennedy)*

- Name one female portrayed on U.S. currency. *(Sacagawea/Susan B. Anthony)*

- What is the word for fake money? *(counterfeit)*

- What is another term for money? *(currency, etc.)*

- What is the place called where coins are produced? *(the Mint)*

- What is the government agency that prints money? *(Treasury)*

## Suggested Reading

- *Alexander, Who Used to Be Rich Last Sunday* by Judith Viorst. Aladdin Paperbacks, 1980.

- *Arthur's TV Trouble* by Marc Brown. Little, Brown and Company, 1997.

- *Blackberry Booties* by Tricia Gardella. Orchard Books, 2000.

- *Boom Town* by Sonia Levitin. Orchard Books, 1998.

- *Bunny Money* by Rosemary Wells. Turtleback, 2002.

- *Count Your Money with the Polk Street School* (Polk Street Special) by Patricial Reilly Giff. Yearling, 1994.

- *Cowries, Coins, Credit: The History of Money* (My Money) by Gerry Bailey and Felicia Law. Compass Point Books, 2006.

- *Dollars* (Welcome Books) by Mary Hill. Children's Press, 2005.

- *How the Second Grade Got $8,205.50 to Visit the Statue of Liberty* by Nathan Zimelman. Albert Whitman & Co., 1992.

- *It's Not Funny, I've Lost my Money!* by Melody Carlson. Crossway Books, 2000.

- *Money* (DK Eyewitness Books) by Joe Cribb and Laura Buller. DK Children, 2005.

- *Money Hungry* by Sharon Flake. Jump at the Sun, 2007.

- *Money Magic Tricks* (Giggle Fit) by Bob Lone. Sterling Publishing, 2001.

- *Money, Money, Honey Bunny* (Bright & Early Books) by Marilyn Sadler and Roger Bollen. Random House, 2006.

- *Pigs Will Be Pigs: Fun with Math and Money* (Aladdin Picture Books) by Amy Axelrod. Aladdin, 1997.

- *Sam & the Lucky Money* by Karen Chinn. Lee & Low Books, 1997.

- *The Story of Money* by Betsy Maestro. Harper Trophy, 1995.

- *The Tortilla Factory* by Gary Paulsen. Voyager Picture Books, 1995.

- *Willimena and the Cookie Money* by Valerie Wilson Wesley. Jump At the Sun, 2001.

## Related Web Sites

- *Brain Pop* (some activities are by registration/fee only), www.brainpop.com/socialstudies/economics/money

- *"Jack and the Bank Stalk" lesson plan about the functions of a bank*, www.usm.edu/english/fairytales/jack/k.htm

- *Kids Bank* (a great site for younger children to learn about money and banking), www.kidsbank.com

- *United States Mint Process*, www.usmint.gov/kids

# Reading Pays!

**Earn $9.99 or more to get a party invitation**

**Penny:** any magazine article

**Nickel:** any EASY book

**Dime:** any book about pigs or money

**Quarter:** Caldecott Award

**$1.00:** any non-fiction book

**$5.00:** any chapter book

**$3.50** biography about a president that is on any currency

Get your earnings from the banker (a.k.a. media specialist) to put into your piggy bank

**Savings Goal: $** ___**$9.99**___     **Investor:**_____

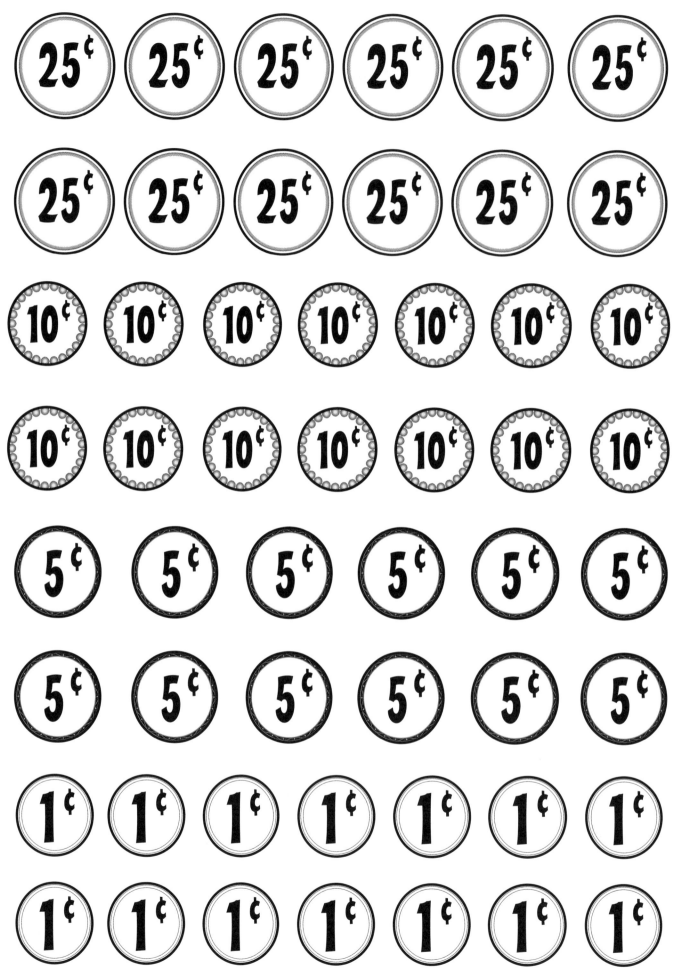

# Reading Pay$!

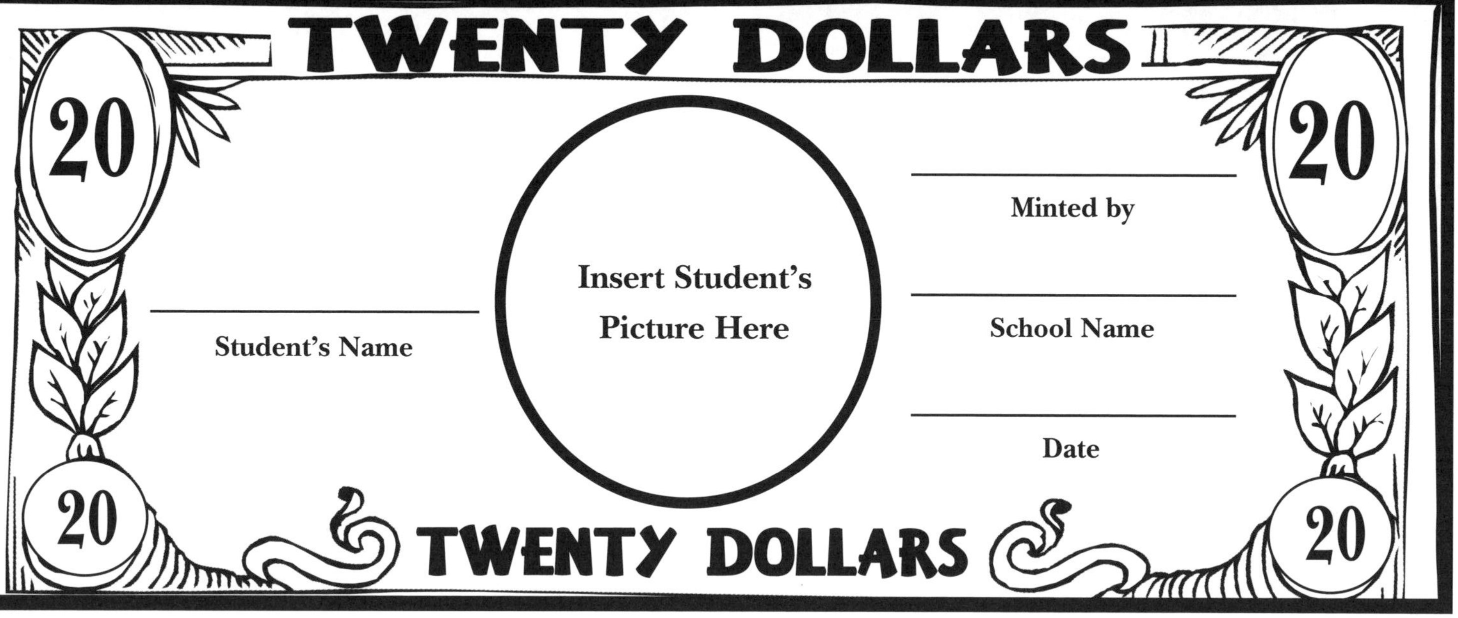

**TWENTY DOLLARS**

20  20

Student's Name

Insert Student's Picture Here

Minted by

School Name

Date

20  20

**TWENTY DOLLARS**

# Reading Pay$!

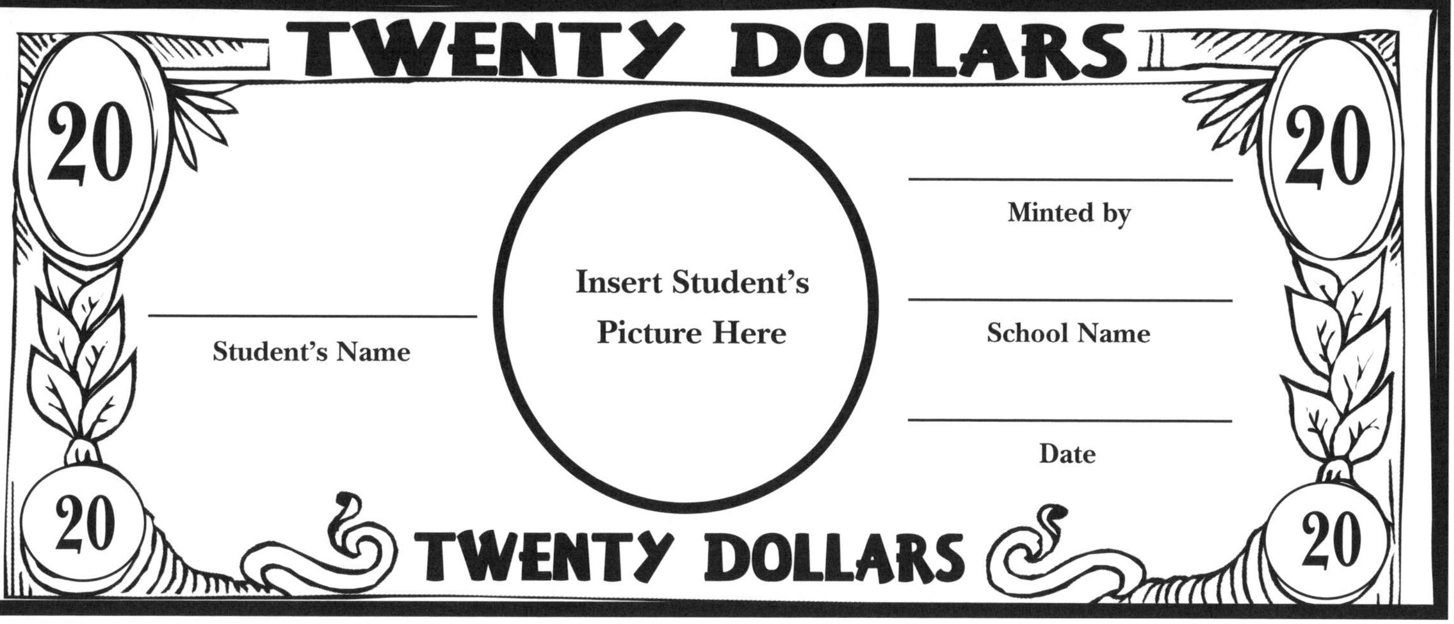

**TWENTY DOLLARS**

20  20

Student's Name

Insert Student's Picture Here

Minted by

School Name

Date

20  20

**TWENTY DOLLARS**

# U.S. Mint Webquest

www.usmint.gov/kids/coinNews/mintingProcess/

Fill in the blanks of the Minting Process using information from the site above; then explore
www.usmint.gov/kids to complete the rest of the questions..

## The Minting Process

| STEP | Process Title | Short Description | New Terms |
|---|---|---|---|
| | Blanking | | |
| | | | Anealing furnace |
| | | The blanks roll through the upsetting mill. | |
| 4 | | | Mottoes striking. |
| 5 | | Press operators inspect the new coins making sure they're ready to roll out of the Mint. | |
| | Counting and Bagging | | |

1.  What does the U.S. Mint do? _____

2.  Where are the U.S. Mint facilities located?_____
    _____

3.  Find the state quarter for the state in which you were born. List three unique features of the quarter. _____

4.  What themes of Abraham Lincoln's life are depicted on the bicentennial Lincoln pennies?

5.  According to the timeline, in what year were cents made out of steel? _____

6.  George Washington was not the first real person to appear on a coin. Who was? _____

7.  Who was the first African American to be featured on a U.S. coin? _____

8.  What is the life expectancy of a circulating coin? (How long does it normally last?)

9.  How long does a paper bill normally last? _____

## Congratulations! You are now RICH in KNOWLEDGE!

# U.S. Mint Webquest

## Answer key

## The Minting Process

| STEP | Process Title | Short Description | New Terms |
|---|---|---|---|
| 1 | Blanking | Round discs are punched out of sheets of metal. | Blanking press, webbing, fabricators |
| 2 | Annealing, Washing, and Drying | Blanks are heated, washed, and dried. | Anealing furnace |
| 3 | Upsetting | The blanks roll through the upsetting mill to raise their rims. | Upsetting mill |
| 4 | Striking | The image of the coin is stamped onto both surfaces. | Mottoes, striking, coining press |
| 5 | Inspecting | Press operators inspect the new coins to make sure they are ready to roll out of the Mint. | Spot-check |
| 6 | Counting and Bagging | Machine counts coins and drops them into canvas bags for distribution. | Pallets |

1. The Mint makes coins and ensures the country has enough coins to carry on daily business.

2. Denver, CO; Fort Knox, KY; Philadelphia, PA; San Francisco, CA; West Point, NY

3. Answers will vary.

4. Birth and Childhood in Kentucky; Youth in Indiana; Professional Life in Illinois; Presidency in Washington, D.C.

5. 1943

6. Abraham Lincoln

7. Booker T. Washington

8. 25 years

9. 18 months

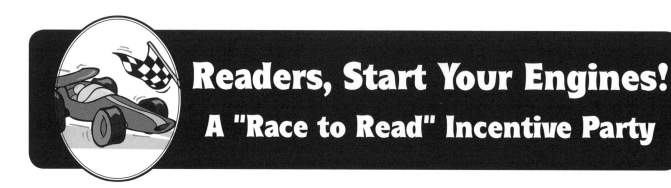

# Readers, Start Your Engines!
## A "Race to Read" Incentive Party

## Incentive Summary

Capitalizing on one of America's favorite pastimes, car racing, proved to be a fun incentive *and* a learning experience. Although my reluctant male readers were the first to be motivated, it didn't take long for every student to *zoom* in and join the race.

This racing-themed incentive encourages students to take the checkered flag by reaching their reading goals, and to keep track of their achievements using a one-page, tri-folded "Ready, Set, READ!" progress tracker (see page 62 for reproducible sample). As with all reading requirements and goals, these can be modified to accommodate individual needs or specific grade levels.

By employing theme-related activities throughout the unit, media specialists and teachers can introduce and incorporate many different concepts. When the day of the party arrives, students who are invited to the "Race to Read" incentive celebration are asked to bring their own remote control cars for a real race around the block. Be sure to have some extras borrowed from elsewhere available. Depending on the number of students attending, tournament brackets may need to be drawn up for competition. Our teacher parking lot happens to be a complete circle, the perfect place for a one-lap race.

Race Day is a highly anticipated event in our school that always gets kids speeding to complete their reading! Who will take the checkered flag?

## Food and Decoration Ideas

- NASCAR Popsicles. This is how we decide who races whom. We buy red, yellow, and green popsicles to represent the "READ" light and have kids choose a popsicle without telling them what the colors mean. After all the students make a selection, the students with the same color popsicles are grouped together. While students are eating their popsicles, hand out certificates (see reproducible sample on page 63), and invite them to step into the Winner's Circle and take their picture.

- Another option if you choose not to do the popsicles is to celebrate with ice cream (Fast Fuel), chocolate syrup (Engine Oil), cherries (Pit Stops), and nuts (Lug Nuts).

## Bulletin Board/Display

Here is a sample of a "Racing Readers"; "Readers, Start Your Engines!"; or "Reading In the Fast Lane!" bulletin board. Get creative! Part of our display included books and theme-related objects about racing, cars, biographies, and the sport of NASCAR. Keep in mind that automotive stores are likely to donate checkered flags and related objects. One of our local auto stores even donated a full-size cardboard stand-up racecar driver that it had on hand for an advertising promotion. We placed a book in the driver's hand!

## Cafeteria Menu

Advertise your incentive program in newsletters, newspapers, and the school Web site. When the whole school participates in an event, students know it must be important. Even the lunchroom can spread a positive atmosphere about the theme. Here are some suggestions:

- Race Car Wheels (hamburgers)
- Pit Crew Pizza
- Gasoline (apple juice)
- Speedy Spaghetti
- Fast Franks (hot dogs)
- Jeff Gordon Goulash (any cafeteria casserole)
- NASCAR'S Nachos
- Zoomin' Soup
- Racing Rancho Beans
- Race Day Ravioli
- Cheering Chicken
- Oreo cookies (black and white and round)
- High Octane Oranges

## Suggested Incentive Activities

- If possible, have a local racecar driver come and speak to the school and bring their race car.
- Visit www.theautochannel.com/sports/allstock/features/nascar_fanclubs.html for addresses and have students write fan letters to their favorite drivers.
- Read biographies of famous (current or former) NASCAR vehicle drivers.
- Have older students (4th/5th grade) design new webquests/games for younger students on the movie "Cars" or any other related idea.
- Using the online catalog, find and categorize books related to racing.
- Make a class Venn diagram comparing/contrasting different circuits of car racing.
- For students during art class: take a model of a NASCAR and modify it with new inventions to make it either faster or safer. Then write a persuasion paragraph telling why yours is a great idea.
- Compare and contrast the movie "Cars" to a nonfiction book on racing.
- Have students complete a webquest on NASCAR (see page 64).
- For a special treat, watch "Herbie: Fully Loaded." Then, have students write a speech persuading others whether or not Herbie should be allowed to enter the professional racing circuit.
- Challenge the principal and assistant principal to race each other if students meet a predetermined reading goal. (What you don't tell them is that they will have to race each other on adult-size tricycles rented by the local party store. Swear the students to secrecy! Shhh!)

- Jokes are another good way to promote what is happening in the media center. It gets kids involved and curious. Morning announcements are a good time to reach out to the whole student population. Promotional advertisements are always a good idea.

  - What does the winner of a race lose? *(his breath)*

  - Why did the barber win the race? *(He knew a short cut.)*

  - How do fireflies start a race? *(Ready, Set, Glow!)*

  - What did the two strings do in the race? *(They tied!)*

  - How do you start a teddy bear race? *(Ready, Teddy, Go!)*

  - What happened when a cabbage, a faucet, and a tomato had a race? *(The cabbage was a-head, the faucet was running, and the tomato was trying to ketch-up!)*

  - What is yellow and fast? *(A banana in a race car)*

## Reference Questions

Have a question of the day on the school intercom, or have a grade-appropriate question displayed during library time and teach students how to find answers. Students can research answers in various ways and turn them in to the media center for prize drawings at the party. Make sure that students document where they found the answer. Use your imagination—this is a great way to portray the importance of the library reference section. Some suggested questions include:

- What does a white flag mean in NASCAR? *(that there is one lap remaining)*

- What is the name of the place where drivers come to refuel and get repairs? *(pit road)*

- What was Janet Guthrie's greatest accomplishment in the sport of racing? *(she was the first woman to complete the Indy 500)*

- Who was the 1999 NASCAR champion? *(Dale Jarrett)*

- What does NASCAR stand for? *(National Association for Stock Car Auto Racing)*

## Suggested Reading

Books should always be available around the bulletin board and/or display for student motivation and reference. Students should also be encouraged to venture outside the school library for further material. Here is a good start for this theme:

- *Brickyard 400* (NASCAR) by Eric Ethan. Gareth Stevens, 1998.

- *Coca-Cola 600* (NASCAR) by Eric Ethan. Gareth Stevens, 1998.

- *Daytona 500* (NASCAR) by Eric Ethan. Gareth Stevens, 1998.

- *Hunger for Racing* by James Douglas. Putnam, 1967.

- *The Greatest Races* by NASCAR. Readers Digest, 2004.

- *Kasey Kahne* (NASCAR Champions) by Connor Dayton. Power Kids Press, 2007.

- *Miller 400* (NASCAR) by Eric Ethan. Gareth Stevens, 1998.

- *NASCAR* (DK Eyewitness Books) by James Buckley. DK Children, 2005.

- *NASCAR ABCs* by Paul D. Jacobs, and Jennifer Swender. Gibbs Smith Publishers, 2007.

- *NASCAR Daring Drivers* (All-Star Readers) by K.C. Kelley. Readers Digest, 2005.

- *NASCAR Pit Pass: Behind the Scenes of NASCAR* by Bob Woods. Readers Digest, 2005.

- *NASCAR Racing to the Finish* (All Star Readers) by K.C. Kelley. Readers Digest, 2005.

- *NASCAR's Wildest Wrecks* by Matt Doeden. Edge Books, 2005.

- *R is for Race: A Stock Car Alphabet* by Brad Herzog. Sleeping Bear Press, 2006.

- *Southern 500* (NASCAR) by Eric Ethan. Gareth Stevens, 1998.

- *Top 10 NASCAR Drivers* by Gail Blasser Riley. Enslow Publishers, Inc., 1995.

- *Winston 500* (NASCAR) by Eric Ethan. Gareth Stevens, 1999.

## Related Web Sites

- *Herbie Fully Loaded (2005)*, www.disney.go.com/disneyvideos/liveaction/herbie

- *Kids Almanac*, www.factmonster.com/ipka/AO768332.html

- *NASCAR fan mail*, www.theautochannel.com/sports/allstock/features/nascar_fanclubs.html

- *NASCAR Official Page*, www.nascar.com

- *Race 2 Learn*, www.race2learn.com

- *Sports Illustrated for Kids*, www.sikids.com/index.html

- *Yahooligans Sports*, www.kids.yahoo.com

# Ready, Set, Read!

**Racer:** _____

You must read on your level and include the following:

1. Nonfiction (2 pts.) _____

2. Biography (2 pts.) _____

3. Your Choice (2 pts.) _____

## Congratulations! You got the checkered flag!

You are invited to the
NASCAR Race Party

Please bring your favorite remote
control car, if you have one.
If you don't, we'll have extras!

# Congratulations, Racing Reader!

_____
Student's Name

_____
Media Specialist

_____
Date

# Congratulations, Racing Reader!

_____
Student's Name

_____
Media Specialist

_____
Date

 # NASCAR Web Quest

## Explore www.nascar.com to complete this Web quest.

1. Locate the NASCAR Glossary. What is the definition of the term, *air dam?*

   _____

2. What is the greatest number of points a driver can earn each race? _____

3. Complete the following chart using your top three favorite drivers.

| Driver | Career Year | Championships | # of starts | # of wins | Total Winnings |
|--------|-------------|---------------|-------------|-----------|----------------|
|        |             |               |             |           |                |
|        |             |               |             |           |                |
|        |             |               |             |           |                |

4. Find the Tracks information section of www.nascar.com and complete the chart below. The first row one is done for you.

| Track Name | Location | Track Length | # of Seats | Draw the Shape of the Track |
|------------|----------|--------------|------------|-----------------------------|
| Martinsville Motor Speedway | Martinsville, Virginia | 0.526 miles | 65,000 | (oval shape drawn) |
| Daytona Beach International Speedway |  |  |  |  |
| Bristol Motor Speedway |  |  |  |  |
| Talladega Super Speedway |  |  |  |  |
| Indianapolis Motor Speedway |  |  |  |  |

 # NASCAR Web Quest

## Answer Key

1. Locate the NASCAR Glossary. What is the definition of the term, *air dam*?

   **A strip that hangs under the front grill close to the ground, which helps provide downforce at the front of the car.**

2. What is the greatest number of points a driver can earn each race? **195**

3. Complete the following chart using your top three favorite drivers. **Answers will vary.**

| Driver | Career Year | Championships | # of starts | # of wins | Total Winnings |
|--------|-------------|---------------|-------------|-----------|----------------|
|        |             |               |             |           |                |
|        |             |               |             |           |                |
|        |             |               |             |           |                |

4. Complete the following chart using www.nascar.com. The first one is done for you.

| Track Name | Location | Track Length | # of Seats | Draw the Shape of the Track |
|------------|----------|--------------|------------|------------------------------|
| **Martinsville Motor Speedway** | Martinsville, Virginia | 0.526 miles | 65,000 | |
| **Daytona Beach International Speedway** | Daytona Beach, FL | 2.5 miles | 168,000 | |
| **Bristol Motor Speedway** | Bristol, TN | .533 miles | 160,000 | |
| **Talladega Super Speedway** | Talladaga, AL | 2.66 miles | 143,231 | |
| **Indianapolis Motor Speedway** | Speedway, IN | 2.5 miles | 30,000 | |

# Shake Your Bookie!

## Incentive Summary

This dance-related theme gets students moving—and reading—by promising lots of fun. The student record for the "Shake Your Bookie!" theme goes hand-in-hand and foot-to-foot with the familiar song, "The Hokey Pokey." (A reproducible sample of the reading record can be found on page 70.) For each verse, students should earn two points in the Accelerated Reader program.

Books they read must be approved by the teacher; be sure to require one biography or nonfiction book about a dancer or dance topic. The amount of points a student earns can be adjusted as needed. Collaborate with teachers on the required amount of reading, and remember to keep the goal attainable, yet challenging. After a parent or teacher quizzes a student about his reading, the adult should sign in the appropriate reading record box. When students complete the entire record, they will receive a party invitation (see reproducible sample on page 71). There are several options for the Shake Your Bookie! theme party, and it may consist of many elements including a reading certificate (see page 72 for reproducible sample). In the past, our students have been invited to watch Disney's High School Musical after completing their reading goal, or to dress up in stylized dance costumes (e.g., clogger, ballerina, country western line dancer, etc.). Boogie Bodies, if funding is available, would be a wonderful way to reward students (see www.boogie-bodies.com). For a less expensive alternative, the media center could host a luau with traditional Hawaiian dancing and party foods, or even a country western ho-down. No matter what you decide, students will be dancing to celebrate their reading accomplishments!

## Food and Decoration Ideas

* Boogie Buns (doughnuts)
* Dance the Dew (Mountain Dew)
* Specific Dance food if option is utilized (such as luau food or country western, etc.)
* Music of all kinds
* A disco ball
* An open floor space in which everyone can dance!

## Bulletin Board/Display

Here is a sample of a "Shake Your Bookie!" bulletin board. Get creative, and be sure to use dance-related book jackets on board. It never fails that the book jackets featured on a bulletin board are the titles that kids ask to check out. Display the board in as prominent a place as possible to keep students motivated and aware of what is going on.

## Cafeteria Menu

Advertise your incentive program in newsletters, newspapers, and the school Web site. When the whole school participates in an event, students know it must be important. Even the lunchroom can spread a positive atmosphere about the theme. Here are some suggestions:

- Ballet Soufflé (any vegetable casserole)
- Break Dancing Breakfast
- Chicken Dance Chicken Strips
- Chips & "Salsa"
- Conga Line Bologna
- Do-Si-"Dough" (biscuits)
- Limbo Linguine (spaghetti)
- Macarena Macaroni
- Swingin' Nachos
- Tap Dance Tacos
- Tater Tot Tutus

## Suggested Incentive Activities

- Have students complete the dance webquest on pages 73–74.
- Read folktales from different countries and teach traditional dance moves from those cultures.
- Instruct students on how to write acrostics with the word "dance."

- Have the local dance team from the high school perform. Also schedule time for them to read their favorite elementary storybook to classes.
- Make dancing Venn diagrams. For instance, compare figure skating to ballet, cheerleading to modern dance, etc.
- Make an alphabet chart for dance-related words with each letter from the alphabet.
- Read biographies of famous dancers, such as Paula Abdul; Elvis; Michael Jackson; Fred Astaire; Anna Pavlova; Patrick Swayze; Sammy Davis, Jr.; John Travolta; Gene Kelley; etc.
- Have groups of students come up with as many styles of dancing as they can in a certain time frame and write them down on chart paper (competition works wonders!).
- Play "dance freeze," a game similar to musical chairs. Turn music on and have everyone dance. When the music stops, students should freeze. Anyone still moving must sit down. The last one standing receives a book prize or extra time in learning centers in the media center.
- In groups, make up a new Library Line Dance.
- As a class, read books about various styles of dance, such as clogging, ballet, tap, square dancing, break dancing, jazz dance, step dancing, belly dancing, etc.
- Coordinate with the P.E. teacher so he or she can teach students different styles of dance.
- Play Library Limbo. Start with the bar way up high for the Dewey 900s. Each increment should move down one more Dewey section. Before play resumes each round, ask students which types of

books are represented in this particular Dewey section.

- Discuss how the rhythm and beat in a song compares to poetry's rhythm and beat.

- Have older students research various careers related to dance. They should then make a job posting for the classifieds that lists Job Title, Job Description, Requirements, Education needed, Salary Range, and Expected Future Growth. Careers might include:

  - Dancer (ballet, modern, jazz)
  - Dance instructor
  - Dance agent
  - Dance or movement therapist
  - Specialized physical therapist
  - Choreographer
  - Costume designer
  - Dance-company manager
  - Dance-studio owner
  - Dance historian
  - Dance critic
  - Dance notator
  - Stage manager
  - Artistic director
  - Arts administrator

- Jokes are a good way to promote what is happening in the media center. It gets kids involved and curious. Morning announcements are an opportune time to reach out to the whole student population. Here are a few that can be read by a student:

  - Why did the man dance in front of the bottle? (*The label said "twist to open."*)

  - Why did the people dance to the vegetable band? (*Because it had a good "beet"*)

  - Where do you dance in California? (*San-FranDISCO*)

  - What is a rabbit's favorite dance style? (*Hip-hop*)

  - What do you get from a dancing cow? (*Milk shakes*)

  - What do you call a dancing sheep? (*A baaaa-lerina*)

  - Who did the monster take to the Halloween dance? (*His ghoul friend*)

  - What is a pretzel's favorite dance? (*The twist*)

## Reference Questions

Have a question of the day on the school intercom, or have a grade-appropriate question displayed during library time and teach students how to find answers. Students can research answers in various ways and turn them in to the media center for prize drawings at the party. Make sure that students document where they found the answer. Use your imagination—this is a great way to portray the importance of the library reference section. Some suggested questions include:

- In dancing terminology, what does it mean to have two left feet? (*clumsy, uncoordinated, etc.*)

- According to the dictionary, how many different parts of speech can the word "dance" be? List them and cite your dictionary source. (*General answer: 3, noun, verb, adjective*)

- What is a full definition of Clog dance? (*Answers may vary; generally speaking, a dance in which clogs, or heavy shoes, are worn for hammering out a lively rhythm.*)

- What 1964 Disney movie features a nanny who dances and teaches the children the word, supercalifragilisticexpialidocious? *(Mary Poppins)*

- What fairytale about a girl who gets her wish to go to dance at the ball? *(Cinderella)*

## Suggested Reading

- *Ballet School* by Naia Bray-Moffatt. DK Children, 2003.

- *Bring it on #1* (Hip –Hop Kidz) by Jasmine Beller. Grosset & Dunlap, 2006.

- *Bust a Move #2* (Hip Hop Kidz) by Jasmine Beller. Grosset & Dunlap, 2006.

- *Dance* (DK Eyewitness Books). DK Publishing, 2005.

- *Dancing to Freedom: The True Story of Mao's Last Dancer* by Li Cunzin. Walker Books for Young Readers, 2008.

- *Go Girl! #7 Dancing Queen* (Go Girl) by Thalia Kalkipsakis. Feiwell and Friends, 2008.

- *A Dictionary of Dance* by Liz Murphy. Blue Apple Books, 2007.

- *Harriet Dancing* by Ruth Symes. The Chicken House, 2008.

- *Let's Hula! Learn to Sway the Hawaiian Way!* by Suzanne Aumack and Connie Majka. Running Press Kids, 2008.

- *Little Ballet Star* by Adele Geras. Dial, 2008.

- *Meadow Dance* by Dennis Rockhill. Raven Tree Press, 2008. Running Kids Press, 2008.

- *Square Dancing* (Let's Dance) by Mark Thomas. Children's Press, 2000.

## Related Web Sites

- *Boogie Bodies*, www.boogie-bodies.com
- *Dance Kids*, www.dance-kids.org

# Do the Hokey Pokey with Books!

## Read, Read, Read

Each verse of the Hokey Pokey is worth two points in A.R. Have a parent or teacher sign in the box to verify you passed your A.R. quiz. Complete the whole song for a party invitation!

# Do The Hokey Pokey With Books!

You put your right foot in,
You put your right foot out,
You put your right foot in,
And you shake it all about,
You do the Hokey Pokey,
And you turn your "book" around,

That's what it's all about!

You put your left foot in,
You put your left foot out,
You put your left foot in,
And you shake it all about,
You do the Hokey Pokey,
And you turn your "book" around,

That's what it's all about!

You put your right hand in,
You put your right hand out,
You put your right hand in,
And you shake it all about,
You do the Hokey Pokey,
And you turn your "book" around,

That's what it's all about!

You put your left hand in,
You put your left hand out,
You put your left hand in,
And you shake it all about,
You do the Hokey Pokey,
And you turn your "book" around,

That's what it's all about!

You put your backside in,
You put your backside out,
You put your backside in,
And you shake it all about,
You do the Hokey Pokey,
And you turn your "book" around,

That's what it's all about!

You put your head in,
You put your head out,
You put your head in,
And you shake it all about,
You do the Hokey Pokey,
And you turn your "book" around,

That's what it's all about!

You put your whole self in,
You put your whole self out,
You put your whole self in,
And you shake it all about,
You do the Hokey Pokey,
And you turn your "book" around,

That's what it's all about!

You're invited to a
Luau because you
shook your bookie!

Guest of Honor:

_____

Homeroom:

_____

**When:** To be announced

**Where:** Playground

**Why:** Because you reached your reading goal!

# Way to go!

See you soon for fun, food, and games!

# I Shook My Bookie!

_____

**Student's Name**

_____

**Signature**

_____

**Date**

# I Shook My Bookie!

_____

**Student's Name**

_____

**Signature**

_____

**Date**

# Dance Webquest

Dancing is a form of personal expression. There are many different types of dances. Explore www.dance-kids.org and then complete the webquest below.

1.  Using the ABCs of dance in the "Lucky Dip" section, fill in the blanks with a style of dance that begins with each letter. The letter "D" example has been done for you.

| | |
|---|---|
| **D** | **Disco** |
| **A** | |
| **N** | |
| **C** | |
| **I** | |
| **N** | |
| **G** | |

2.  Name three traditional Polish Dances as explained in the "Dancing Globe" section.

    _____

    _____

    _____

3.  To what address would you send a dance-related picture or photo?

    _____

4.  Print out either the crazy maze or wicked words and complete. Turn in with your webquest. (Do NOT complete online.)

5.  What is the oldest form of Swedish dance?

    _____

6.  Choose one style of dancing based on the types listed in the ABCs of Dance. Research the style and write one paragraph summary of it on a separate sheet of paper. Turn in with your webquest.

# Dance Webquest

## Answer Key

1. Using the ABCs of dance in the "Lucky Dip" section, fill in the blanks with a style of dance that begins with each letter. The letter "D" example has been done for you.

   **Note: Some letters may have more than one answer; verify with Web site**

| | |
|---|---|
| **D** | **Disco** |
| **A** | **Alternative Rhythms** |
| **N** | **National Dance** |
| **C** | **Cha Cha** |
| **I** | **Irish Dancing** |
| **N** | **National Dance** |
| **G** | **Greek** |

2. Name three traditional Polish Dances as explained in the "Dancing Globe" section.

   **Answers include: Chodzony, Mazurka, Polonaise, Polka**

3. To what address would you send a dance-related picture or photo?

   **Dance-Kids Gallery**
   **ISTD Dance Examinations Board**
   **Imperial House**
   **22/26 Paul Street**
   **London EC 2 4QE**

   **ENGLAND**

4. Print out either the crazy maze or wicked words and complete. Turn in with your webquest. (Do NOT complete online.)

5. What is the oldest form of Swedish dance?

   **The Circle or Chain Formation**

6. Choose one style of dancing based on the types listed in the ABCs of Dance. Research the style and write one paragraph summary of it on a separate sheet of paper. Turn in with your webquest.

# Wanted: Readers!

## Incentive Summary

Put on your ten-gallon hats, because this is a western theme! Students are taught about the western states and the history of cowboys and cowgirls throughout this month-long unit. They read or risk being locked up by the town Sheriff (the principal), and they get to kick up their spurs a little at the O.K. Corral party when they achieve their reading goal.

Have students earn their invitation to the party at the O.K. Corral by requiring them to read one (teacher-approved) biography or nonfiction book related to the western theme, as well as other requirements. Collaborate with teachers on the required amount of reading. It should vary for individual grades, and remember to keep the goal attainable, yet challenging. Students can keep track of their reading with a progress tracker (for reproducible sample, see page 79). Send incentive party invitations to those students who reach their goal or reading requirement. A reproducible invitation sample is available on page 80.

After invitations are sent out, students will want to mosey on down to the O.K. Corral (library, gym, etc.) for a Texas-size good time, or it can be arranged to pick them up in a stage coach (a.k.a. hay ride) and delivered to the local park. Students should be encouraged to dress up like cowboys or cowgirls on the day of the party, where food will be served and cowpoke games will be played!

Games might include:

- Horseshoes
- Race Your (stick) Horse Relay around barrels
- Dress Your Cowpoke Relay Races (have pieces like bandana, cowboy hats, vests, boots, and chaps on hand for relay-teams compete to get dressed one piece at a time)
- Watermelon seed-spitting contest

Have book-related prizes for awards. Hand out certificates and make sure to take lots of pictures for the school scrapbook.

## Food and Decoration Ideas

- The party at the OK Corral should include western decorations bought at any party supply store or www.oriental-trading.com.
- Food might include a boot-shaped cake decorated with, "Boot Scootin' with Books!"
- Sasparilla (root beer)
- Trail Mix
- Watermelon

## Bulletin Board/Display

Here is a sample of a Wanted: Readers! bulletin board. Get creative! For another display, begin a "Caught Reading" or "Captured Reading" display, with a few posters featuring various staff members. For instance, snap a photo of the principal reading, and beneath the photo, list facts about the principal's reading habits (e.g.,

NAME: Mrs. Adams CAUGHT READING: At her desk during lunchtime NAME OF BOOK: *Thirteenth Child* by Patricia Wrede OFFICIAL STATEMENT: "I'm only on page 17 and I'm already hooked! I can't wait to see how this turns out!"). Have younger and older students add to this display (see details in Suggested Incentive Activities section below).

## Cafeteria Menu

Advertise your incentive program in newsletters, newspapers, and the school Web site. When the whole school participates in an event, students know it must be important. Even the lunchroom can spread a positive atmosphere about the theme. Here are some suggestions:

- Rancho beans
- Stampede Spaghetti
- Get Along Grits
- Tater Skins
- Gallopin' Corn Fritters
- Trail Herdin' Pizza
- Sasparilla (root beer)
- Cowboy Cuisine (meat casserole)
- Saddle Down Chicken
- Boot Scootin' BBQ
- Classic Western Chili

- Western Dumplings
- Cow Patties (chocolate oatmeal cookies)
- Roasted Corn on the Cob
- Western Omelettes

## Suggested Incentive Activities

- Have students complete the Wanted: Readers! webquest on page 81–82.
- Have students conduct group research to locate as many animals as they can with the name "western" in it. See page 83 for a partial list.
- Geography lesson: As a class, have students identify the individual states that collectively make up what is commonly referred to as "the West."
- Read *Armadillo Rodeo* by Jan Brett (Putnam, 1995) and then visit her Web site at www.janbrett.com for related activities.
- Make trail mix using an assembly line. Depending on food allergies, add pretzels, peanuts, skittles, raisins, marshmallows, M&Ms, etc.). Students can individually graph their ingredients.
- Ask the P.E. or music teacher to teach students how to line dance.
- Discuss various elements of a cowboy's costume. Why do they need these pieces? What purposes do rope, chaps, spurs, boots, a bandana, and hats serve?
- Divide famous western characters into those on the wrong and right sides of the law. Discuss nicknames, such as the Sundance Kid. Does that give it away? What research book can help you decide which category to put each person in?

- Have students create their own wanted posters to add to the display idea described earlier in the chapter. For example, WANTED READER (student makes up his/her own nickname), WANTED FOR (crime), LAST SEEN, REWARD. Have students in upper grades continue making posters of various staff members for your "Captured Reader"/ "Caught Reading" display.

- Define and discuss branding. Using online reference tools, as a class, locate five different famous brands. Trace the brands onto a sponge and cut them out. Attach the brands to a dowel rod with hot glue. Have students dip the dowel into paint and "brand" various spots on chart paper that you have hung on the wall.

- Watch the Reading Rainbow episode, "Meanwhile, Back at the Ranch."

- Change the words to Ten Little Indians to Ten Little Cowboys or Cowgirls. Have student groups work together and then perform.

- Play Pin the Hat on the Cowboy.

- Designate a Friday where students can dress up as cowboys or cowgirls. The principal (Sheriff) can lock up students if she catches them reading. Being locked up, though, would be a good thing; students could be awarded time in the media center for "Rodeo Round-up with Book Time."

- Make western dioramas.

- "Yippee Ki-yi-yay!" jokes are a good way to promote what is happening in the media center. It gets kids involved and curious. Morning announcements are an opportune time to reach out to the whole student population. Here are a few that can be read by a student:

  - How did the cowboy ride into town on Friday, stay for three days, and ride out again on Friday? (*His horse's name was Friday.*)

  - What do you call a happy cowboy? (*A jolly rancher*)

  - Why did the cowboy buy a daschund? (*He wanted to get a long little doggie.*)

  - What did the cowboy say when the bear ate Lassie? (*Well, doggone!*)

  - Why did the cowboy's horse have to gargle with mouthwash? (*Because he was a little horse*)

  - What did the cowboy's horse say when he fell? (*I've fallen and I can't giddy-up*)

  - What do you call a cowboy and his horse that lives next door? (*A "neigh"-bor*)

  - Why did the cowboy cross the road with his horse? (*Because the chicken needed a day off*)

## Reference Questions

Have a question of the day on the school intercom, or have a grade-appropriate question displayed during library time and teach students how to find answers. Students can research answers in various ways and turn them in to the media center for prize drawings at the party. Make sure that students document where they found the answer. Use your imagination—this is a great way to portray the importance of the library reference section. Some suggested questions include:

- What was famous cowboy, Hop-along Cassidy's real name? (*William Boyd*)

- What is the definition of a drugstore cowboy? (*A person who passes time on sidewalks, or one who dresses or acts like a cowboy but has never been one)*

- What famous book by Lynne Reid Banks is about a little wooden cabinet, a toy cowboy, and a Native American figurine? *(The Indian in the Cupboard)*

- What president of the United States was also an actor and played several roles as a cowboy in movies? *(Ronald Reagan)*

- What was famous cowboy Roy Rogers's horse's name? *(Trigger)*

- How many books does your media center have that contains the word "west" in it? *(Students must use their online catalog; answers will vary.)*

## Suggested Reading

- *B is for Buckaroo: A Cowboy Alphabet* by Louise Doak Whitney and Gleaves Whitney. Sleeping Bear Press, 2003.

- *Buster Goes to Cowboy Camp* by Denise Fleming. Henry, Holt & Company, 2008.

- *C is for Cowboy: A Wyoming Alphabet Edition 1* (Discover America State by State) by Eugene Gagliano. Sleeping Bear Press, 2003.

- *Cowboy Camp* by Tammi Sauer. Sterling Publishing, 2005.

- *Cowboy Small* by Lois Lenski. Random House Books for Young Readers, 2001.

- *Cowboys* (Library of Congress Classics) by Martin Sandler. Harper Trophy, 2000.

- *Cowboys and Cowgirls: YippeeYay!* by Gail Gibbons. Little, Brown Young Readers, 2003.

- *The Dirty Cowboy* by Amy Timberlake and Adam Rex. Farrar, Straus and Giroux (BYR), 2003.

- *Eyewitness: Cowboy* (Eyewitness Books) by David S. Murdoch. DK Children, 2000.

- *The Gingerbread Cowboy* by Janet Squires. Laura Geringer Books, 2006.

- *Old Chisholm Trail: A Cowboy Song* by Rosalyn Schanzer. National Geographic Children's Books, 2001.

- *The Toughest Cowboy: or How the Wild West was Tamed* (Bccb Blue Ribbon Picture Book Awards (Awards)) by John Frank. Simon & Schuster Children's Publishing, 2004.

## Related Web Sites

- *American West information*, www.ameri canwest.com

- *Howdy, Partner! Unit*, www.thevir tualvine.com/cowboys.html (www. thevirtualvine.com is great website for teachers with lots of units and other related links)

- *National Cowboy Museum*, www.cow boykids.nationalcowboymuseum.org

- *Oregon Trail information*, www.isu.edu/ ~trinmich/oregontrail.html

# WANTED: READERS!

## Lasso Up Some Books!

**Directions:** Every time you read for an hour, have your parent or teacher sign in the box. When you have all of your cowboy/western supplies, you will be invited to the party at the O.K. Corral!

Your Name: _____

# Invitation Sample

**WANTED: YOU!**

**You are invited to a Wanted Readers party at the O.K. Corral!**

Where:

When:

Why: Because YOU are a rootin', tootin' reader!

**Don't forget to dress up as a cowboy or cowgirl before you mosey on down to the corral!**

# Wanted: Readers Webquest

## National Cowboy & Western Heritage Museum
### http://cowboykids.nationalcowboymuseum.org

**Directions:** Explore the Web site above, and use it to help you complete the webquest below.

1. Where is the National Cowboy and Western Heritage Museum located?

   _____

2. Visit the Image Archive on the Research Center page. Who painted the picture titled "Branding JJ"? _____

3. Visit the Canyon Princess sculpture on the Diamond R Ranch Sculpture Tour. How much does it weigh and what is it made of?

   _____

4. Take the Diamond R Ranch Sculpture Tour and write down the name of the statue that greets visitors from the top of Persimmon Hill. _____

5. Which sculpture does the tour identify as one of the most recognized symbols of the American West?

   _____

6. Visit the Exhibits section. What does a cowboy use a Sourdough Keg for? _____

7. What is another word for a cowboy's rope? _____

8. What do chaps protect the cowboy from? _____

10. Describe the six cowboy characters on the wagon train.

   _____
   _____
   _____
   _____
   _____

# "Wanted: Readers" Web Quest

## Answer Key

1. Where is the National Cowboy and Western Heritage Museum located?
   Oklahoma City, Oklahoma

2. Visit the Image Archive on the Research Center page. Who painted the picture titled "Branding JJ"? William R. Leigh

3. Visit the Canyon Princess sculpture on the Diamond R Ranch Sculpture Tour. How much does it weigh and what is it made of? Eight tons and yule marble

4. Take the Diamond R Ranch Sculpture Tour and write down the name of the statue that greets visitors from the top of Persimmon Hill. "The Westerner"

5. Which sculpture does the tour identify as one of the most recognized symbols of the American West? "End of the Trail"

6. Visit the Exhibits section. What does a cowboy use a Sourdough Keg for?

   This container was very important to the chuck wagon cook. A portion of the contents (a mixture of sour milk, sugar, and yeast) was mixed with flour to make sourdough biscuits. The cowboys always wanted biscuits with their coffee. Only the cook was willing to work with the starter mix in the keg because it smelled so bad. Sometimes the cook would sleep with the keg to keep it warm.

7. What is another word for a cowboy's rope?
   Lasso or lariat

8. What do chaps protect the cowboy from?
   Heavy brush and rope burns

9. In the game Help the Boys, what does Cowboy Waddie need and why?
   A book because they had to pack lightly and a book was considered entertainment

10. Describe the six cowboy characters on the wagon train.

| | |
|---|---|
| Cowboy Jack, the Trail Boss | Dusty Trails, the Top Hand |
| Zeke, the Trail Herdin' Cowboy | Sing Song, the Camp Cook |
| Waddie, the Poem Recitin' Cowboy | Joaquin, the Primero Vaquero |

# "Western" Animals

Western Banded Gecko

Western Spadefoot

Western King Bird

Western Tanager

Western Patch-Nosed Snake

Western Diamondback Rattlesnake

Western Fence Lizard

Western Hognose Snake

Western Worm Snake

Western Swamp Turtle

Western Screech Owl

Western Toad

Western Terrestrial Garter Snake

Western Pond Turtle

Western Skink

Western Scrub Jay

Western Coral Snake

Western Shovel-nosed Snake

Western Ribbon Snake

Western Blend Snake

*(add to list as necessary)*

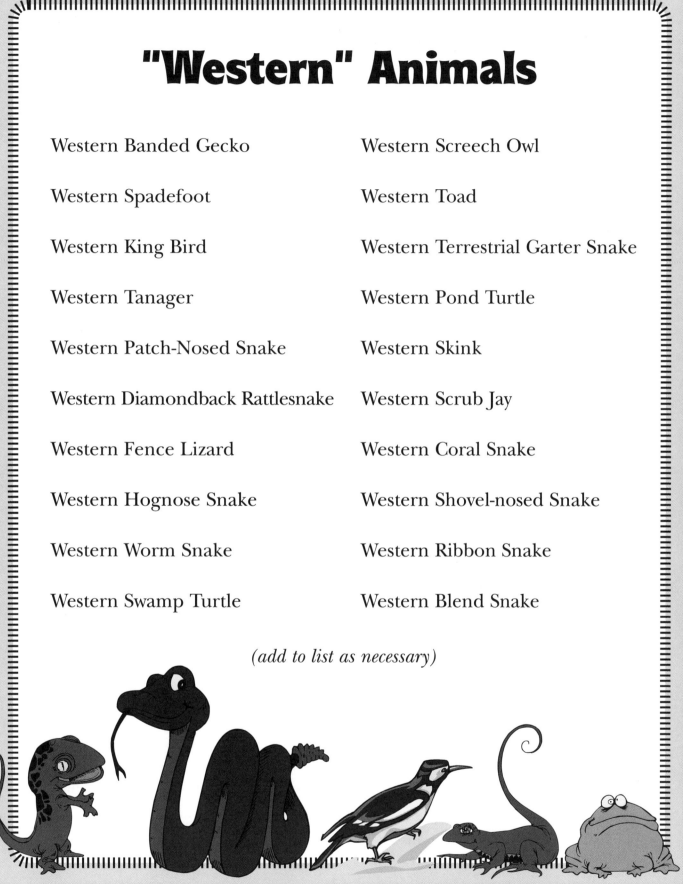

# For Goodness "Snakes," READ!

## Incentive Summary

This snake-related incentive was borne of a bargain I made with a student several years ago. The student jokingly told me he would finish a chapter book I suggested to him if I would agree to hold his pet garter snake. Of course, he didn't realize that no one should bet me when it comes to getting students to read! He brought in his garter snake, I held it, and he had to finish reading the book. Through this experience, I was able to get to know this student a bit better, and was eventually able to point out books that he might enjoy. Gradually, he began to appreciate books more and more. And if that wasn't a satisfying enough result, the idea for a new motivational party emerged, too—and today, it is one of our most popular!

While this unit can be accommodated for any grade level, I have found that my third–fifth grade students participate the most and seem to have the most fun. While in the media center, students are exposed to snake-related activities that cover objectives across the curriculum. To be invited to the Snake Party at the end of the month (see page 88 for reproducible invitation sample), students must earn the privilege. For example, kindergartners may have to read 20 books at home and have appropriate documentation to show for it. Fourth grade students may have to accumulate ten points in the accelerated reader program on their reading level. Other appropriate reading goals can be established based on the individual student, class, or school. See page 89 for a reproducible reading record sample; students will be required to have an adult sign off on each segment of the snake as they progress with their reading goals.

The culminating snake celebration can take many forms. One year, we invited a representative from the Georgia Reptile and Amphibian Rescue Effort—as well as some of his scaly friends—to visit. He brought snakes, turtles, and lizards for students to meet. The 6-foot boa constrictor was their unquestionable favorite. Another idea is to celebrate at your local zoo, with a special presentation by the zoo's herpetologist. (The herpetologist is also someone you might contact to speak at your party, if you choose to hold it at school.) Party activities might include the Snakes and Ladders board game, team snake jeopardy (formulate questions based on snake facts and required reading), and a Snake in the Grass Hunt, in which students search for rubber snakes within a designated area (prizes might be a No Homework Night, an extra book to check out, gift certificate to a book store, etc.). Rubber snakes are easily purchased at toy stores and at Web sites such as www.orientaltrading.com. A certificate of achievement is always a nice addition; a reproducible sample can be found on page 90.

## Food and Decoration Ideas

- Snake cake: a large sheet cake covered in gummy snakes, or two circle cakes cut in half (use a bundt pan or a circular pan), with the four segments arranged end-to-end and frosted in green

- Snake ring-chain decorations made from colorful strips of paper taped into chain links

- Green and yellow plates, napkins, and tablecloths

- Rocks or small plants on tables with rubber snakes placed on them

## Bulletin Board/Display

Here is a sample of a For Goodness "Snakes," READ! bulletin board. Get creative! Consider decorating the border with dozens of paper or rubber snakes (available at a low cost at www.orientaltrading.com and other party vendors).

For a display, you might arrange a dozen or so books about snakes and reptiles from your collection in a serpentine pattern across a bookshelf, the circulation desk, or some other highly visible place. At the "head" of the book snake, create a paper snake face and a sign that says, "For Goodness "Snakes," READ!" Try to pull all genres to reach every age and interest.

## Cafeteria Menu

Advertise your incentive program in newsletters, newspapers, and the school Web site. When the whole school participates in an event, students know it must be important. Even the lunchroom can spread a positive atmosphere about the theme. Here are some suggestions:

- Snake Dogs (regular hot dogs with two sliced black olives for eyes)

- "Hissing" Ham

- RattleBurgers (regular hamburgers)

- Cobra Casserole (any casserole will suffice)

- Slithering Spaghetti

- Scaly Pizza (regular pizza with scattered corn flakes on top)

- Snake Eggs (scrambled eggs dyed green)

- Turtle eggs (whole boiled potatoes)

- Lizard Legs (small fried chicken legs)

- Gummy snakes for dessert

## Suggested Incentive Activities

- Have students complete the writing activity entitled "My Hissstory as a Snake."

- Direct students to team up in groups of four and assign each group a snake to research (cobra, rattlesnake, mamba, cottonmouth, garter snake, etc.). They should take note of the snake's average length, diet, habitat, lifespan, threat level to humans, etc. Then, have students compare and contrast their snake species using a large Venn diagram.

- Assign a species of snake to each student and have them research the location of their snakes' habitats. Post a world map on the wall, and have each student identify the location with a pushpin and share two facts about the species they researched.

- Student Library Hunt finding fiction and non-fiction literature about snakes/reptiles

- Introduce students to the bi-colored-python-rock-snake of Rudyard Kipling's *Just So Stories*.

- Make a snake! Give each student a knee-high stocking and have them stuff it with cotton. Then, allow them to browse books featuring snakes, and provide them with paints and brushes to decorate their "sock snake" whatever colors they imagine.

- Have students complete the word search on page 91.

- Jokes are a good way to promote what is happening in the media center. It gets kids involved and curious. Morning announcements are an opportune time to reach out to the whole student population. Here are a few that can be read by a student:

  – What do snakes and George Washington have in common? *(They're both hisssssssstory.)*

  – What did the naughty little diamondback say to his big sister? *("Don't be such a rattle-tail!")*

  – What kind of snake can drive cars? *(Ana-Honda)*

  – Why can't you play jokes on snakes? *(Because you can't pull their legs.)*

  – What do you get when you cross a snake and a kangaroo? *(A jump rope!)*

  – What do you call a snake without any clothes on? *(Snaked!)*

  – Why did the snake cross the road? *(To get to the other sssssssside.)*

## Reference Questions

Have a question of the day on the school intercom, or have a grade-appropriate question displayed during library time and teach students how to find answers. Students can research answers in various ways and turn them in to the media center for prize drawings at the party. Make sure that students document where they found the answer. Use your imagination—this is a great way to portray the importance of the library reference section. Some suggested questions include:

- What is the scientific name for the giant garter snake? (*Thamnophis gigas*)

- What is the name for a person who studies reptiles and amphibians? (A herpetologist)

- Why do snakes shed their skin? (Allows snake to rid itself of parasites; old skin gets worn down, etc.)

- According to Greek mythology, who was Medusa? (Answers may vary; generally considered a female monster with snakes for hair who could turn onlookers into stone)

- The snake symbolizes different things in cultures around the world. What are three characteristics that the snake has come to represent? (Answers will vary and may include: wisdom, trickery, healing, poison, guardianship, etc.)

## Suggested Reading

- *Baseball, Snakes, and Summer Squash: Poems About Growing Up* by Donald Graves and Paul Berling. Boyds Mills Press, 1996.

- *Cam Jansen & the Scary Snake Mystery* by David Adler. Puffin, 2005.

- *Snake* by Chris Mattison. DK Publishing, 2006.

- *Snakes* by Seymour Simon. Collins, 2007.

- *The Snake Scientist* by Sy Montgomery. Houghton Mifflin, 2001.

- *Turtle & Snake Go Camping* by Kate Spohn. Puffin, 2000.

## Related Web Sites

- *The 10 Deadliest Snakes*, library.thinkquest.org/05aug/01812

- *The Amazing World of Reptiles*, library.thinkquest.org/04oct/00246

- *Slithering Snakes*, library.thinkquest.org/CR0213183

- *Snakes!* library.thinkquest.org/J0111684

- *Snakes of North America*, www.pitt.edu/~mcs2/herp/SoNA.html

- *What you always wanted to know about snakes*, library.thinkquest.org/5409

- *Yahooligans Site for the Scavenger Hunt*, www.yahooligans.yahoo.com/snakes

# You're Invited to a Snake Celebration!

**Where:**

**When:**

**Why:**   Because you are a sssssspectacular reader!

# You're Invited to a Snake Celebration!

**Where:**

**When:**

**Why:**   Because you are a sssssspectacular reader!

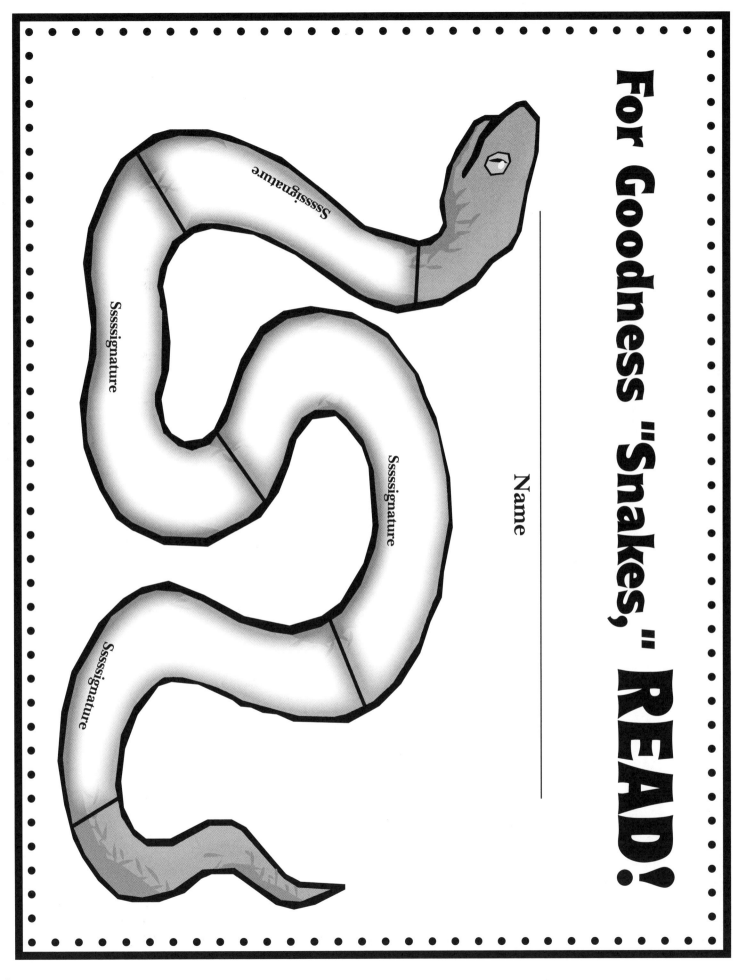

For Goodness "Snakes," READ!

Name

Ssssignature

Sssssignature

Ssssssignature

Ssssssignature

# You're a Sssssuper Reader!

_____

**Name**

# You're a Sssssuper Reader!

_____

**Name**

# Snake Wordsearch

```
D L Y S A O I T O O P F Q S H
E A O G E N G Y I T K R N R U
D E P O O L A I P Q U S E H G
O S L J H L A C A W B N T Y F
O E Q W U R O C O V D U A M I
L R O T C I R T S N O C A O B
B P Z H W D B L E M D V Y N V
D E I J Q I I N N P Z A P E H
L N H Y C T U O Z P R G I V N
O T L N H G T S H E D E R O S
C B J E I T X G Q E W L H I T
O L R C O R A L S N A K E S K
K A Y C E L I T P E R M S U L
E J R N Z C E Y B F E I H L B
U C I Q L E D L Y G H N S V Q
```

| | | |
|---|---|---|
| boa constrictor | scales | cold blooded |
| serpent | shed | cottonmouth |
| venom | reptile | coral snake |
| slither | herpetology | anaconda |
| hiss | prey | |

# B.E.A.R.
## (Be Enthusiastic About Reading!)

## Incentive Summary

What better to snuggle up with while you're reading than a teddy bear? Ever since President Roosevelt refused to shoot a captured baby bear back in 1902, "teddy bears" have been popular with kids. Thus in our library was born the Teddy Bear month. To capitalize on this love of the cuddly stuffed animals, we initiated a motivational unit incentive to get kids to read, read, and read!

While this unit can be accommodated for any grade level, I have had the most fun and participation with my K–2 students.

To be invited to the Teddy Bear Party at the end of the month, students have to earn it. For example, kindergartners may have to read twenty books at home and have appropriate documentation to show for it. One way that we have done this in the past to give them a Bear Bookmark Reading Record (see page 96 for reproducible sample) to keep up with their books. Every book that they read earns a grownup's initials. Fourth grade students may have to accumulate ten points in the Accelerated Reader program on their reading level. The media specialist should keep in mind to always make the goal obtainable. The object is to have students motivated enough to read but able to successfully reach the goal too. During the month while students are working independently on their reading goals, we have Teddy Bear activities in the media center (see the suggested list later in this chapter). The media

center "Bear" activities tend to cover objectives that span across the curriculum.

At the end of the month we celebrate those students who have reached their goal. According to the theme of the month and the number of participants, I decide whether I want to break the parties into grade levels. After assembling the guest list, each student receives a Teddy Bear Invitation (see page 97 for reproducible sample) to the party. We ask students to also bring their favorite teddy bear with them, and we have circle time to allow students to "show and tell" about their own teddy. When our principal shows her teddy bear that she had when she was a little girl, the kids think it is "100 YEARS OLD!"

After we have our show and tell, we go on a Teddy Bear Parade around the school. This is always a fun time because the students get to show off their hard work. We also have a group picture as well as individual pictures for the school scrapbook. Each student is given a certificate to commemorate this special event (see page 98 for reproducible sample), and we cap it all off with a showing of The Library Store's movie of the Vermont Teddy Bear Factory, so students can see how a teddy bear is made.

## Food and Decoration Ideas

- Teddy Bears' Picnic Theme: lemonade, teddy bear suckers, gummy bears, a teddy bear cake, and picnic sandwiches

- Teddy bears, teddy bears, everywhere! Teddy bear decorations can be bought at most any party supply store or www.orientaltrading.com.

## Bulletin Board/Display

Here is a sample of a B.E.A.R. bulletin board. Get creative and cuddly! Consider using the B.E.A.R. slogan as well as others, such as, "READY, TEDDY?"

Around the bulletin board we exhibit all of our books that go along with teddy bears or related materials. I try to pull all genres to reach every age and interest. We also display fun props, such as honey, honeybees, etc.

## Cafeteria Menu

Advertise your incentive program in newsletters, newspapers, and the school Web site. When the whole school participates in an event, students know it must be important. Even the lunchroom can spread a positive atmosphere about the theme. Here are some suggestions:

- BEAR-b-que sandwiches
- HamBEARgers
- BlueBEARY muffins
- Gummi BEARS
- Teddy Grahams

## Suggested Incentive Activities

- Make teddy bear masks. See page 99 for a reproducible pattern.
- "Bear-Nap" students who are caught reading; they receive a sticker and get to come to the library for "beary" special activities.
- Have students research details about famous bears, such as Smokey, Yogi, and President Roosevelt's teddy bear.
- Assign bear-related writing prompts: ("The day I ran from a grizzly . . . " "My pet bear cub . . . ")
- Play Bear Bingo using gummy bears with your regular Bingo game.
- Compare and Contrast various species of bears (Alaska Brown Bear, Polar Bear, American Black Bear, Grizzly Bear, etc.).
- Have students complete the Name that Famous Bear worksheet on page 100. Answers are below:

  1. Who was the mascot of the U.S. Forest Fire Prevention Campaign who first appeared in 1944? (*Smokey Bear*)

  2. What Teddy Bear came from Darkest Peru and usually wears a blue coat and yellow hat? (*Paddington Bear*)

  3. What bear was featured in a series of books illustrated by Maurice Sendak? (*Little Bear*)

  4. What was the name of the bear of the famous rhyme that had no hair? (*Fuzzy Wuzzy*)

  5. Name the three bears that Goldilocks encountered in the woods. (*Mama Bear, Papa Bear, and Baby Bear*)

  6. What is the group of bears called that includes: Bedtime Bear, Birth-

day Bear, Cheer Bear, Share Bear, Good Luck Bear, etc.? (*The Care Bears*)

7. What are the names of the bears that live in JellyStone Park and have their own cartoon? (*Yogi Bear, Boo Boo Bear, and Cindy Bear*)

8. What is the name of the bear that appeared in Disney's animated classic, "The Jungle Book"? (*Baloo*)

9. What famous, shy, yellow bear is also a classic Disney character and has a friend named Piglet? (*Winnie-the-Pooh*)

- Assign a species of bear to each student and have them research the location of their bears' habitats. Post a world map on the wall, and have each student identify the location with a pushpin and share two facts about the species they researched.

- Jokes are a good way to promote what is happening in the media center. It gets kids involved and curious. Morning announcements are an opportune time to reach out to the whole student population. Here are a few that can be read by a student:

  - What did Teddy Bear's friends say to him after he had blown out the candles on his cake? (*HAPPY BEARTHDAY!*)

  - Where do teddy bears go to get books? (*The li-BEAR-y*)

  - What famous teddy bear was born in a log and became president of the United States? (*A-BEAR-ham Lincoln!*)

  - How do you start a Teddy Bear race: (*Teddy, Set, GO!*)

  - How do Teddies keep their houses cool in summer? (*They use BEAR conditioning!*)

  - What animal do you look like when you get into the bath? (*A little bear!*)

  - What did the Teddy Bear say when he was offered a second helping? (*No thanks, I'm already stuffed!*)

## Reference Questions

Have a question of the day on the school intercom, or have a grade-appropriate question displayed during library time and teach students how to find answers. Students can research answers in various ways and turn them in to the media center for prize drawings at the party. Make sure that students document where they found the answer. Use your imagination—this is a great way to portray the importance of the library reference section. Some suggested questions include:

- What is the Latin name for the constellation called the Great Bear? (*Ursa Major*)

- What is the name for a person who studies bears? (*An ursinologist*)

- What is the smallest species of bear in the world? (*The Malayan sun bear*)

- What is a polar bear's primary source of food? (*Seals*)

## Suggested Reading

- The Berenstain Bears series by Stan and Jan Berenstain, from HarperCollins.

- *The Boy Who Thought He Was a Teddy Bear: A Fairy Tale* by Jeanne Willis. Peachtree Press, 2002.

- Corduroy books by Don Freeman, from Viking.

- *How Teddy Bears are Made: A Visit to the Vermont Teddy Bear Factory* by Ann Morris. Scholastic, 1994.

- *The Legend of the Teddy Bear* by Frank Murphy. Sleeping Bear Press, 2000.

- *Teddy Bear, Teddy Bear: Poems* by Alice Schertle. HarperCollins, 2003.

- *Teddy Bears Picnic* by Jerry Garcia. HarperCollins, 1996.

- *The Story of Smokey Bear* by Robin Bromley. Dutton, 1996.

- *A Tale of Two Teddies* by Kathleen Bart. Portfolio Press, 2001.

- *A Teddy Bear for President Roosevelt* by Peter and Connie Roop. Scholastic Book Clubs, 2002.

- *The True Story of Smokey the Bear* by Jane W. Watson. Simon & Schuster, 1955.

- *Ultimate Teddy Bear Book* by Pauline Cockrill. DK Publishing, 1991.

- *When the Teddy Bears Came* by Martin Waddell. Walker Books, 1998.

- *Who Wants an Old Teddy Bear?* by Ginnie Hofmann. Random House, 1979.

## Related Web Sites

- *Smokey Bear*, www.smokeybear.com/kids

- *Walt Disney's Winnie-the-Pooh*, disney. go.com/disneyvideos/animatedfilms/ pooh/

- *Theodore Roosevelt Association: Teddy and the Children's Room*, theodoreroosevelt. org/kidscorner/trchildrens.htm

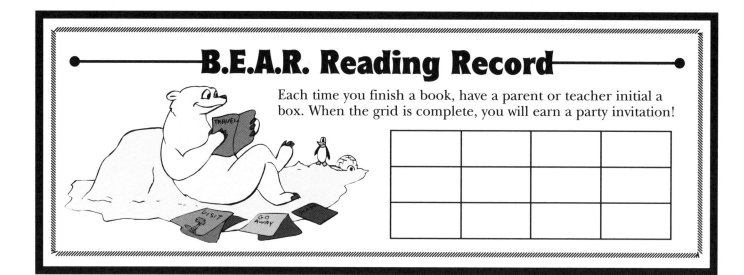

# B.E.A.R. Reading Record

Each time you finish a book, have a parent or teacher initial a box. When the grid is complete, you will earn a party invitation!

# B.E.A.R. Reading Record

Each time you finish a book, have a parent or teacher initial a box. When the grid is complete, you will earn a party invitation!

# B.E.A.R. Reading Record

Each time you finish a book, have a parent or teacher initial a box. When the grid is complete, you will earn a party invitation!

# It's a Teddy Bear Party!

**Where:**

**When:**

**Why:**

Make sure to bring your favorite teddy bear!

# It's a Teddy Bear Party!

**Where:**

**When:**

**Why:**

Make sure to bring your favorite teddy bear!

# You're a "Beary" Special Reader!

_____

**Name**

_____
**Signature**

_____
**Date**

# You're a "Beary" Special Reader!

_____

**Name**

_____
**Signature**

_____
**Date**

# Make a Bear Mask

1. Decorate and/or color this bear.

2. Cut the eyes and the face out.

3. Tape a craft stick to the back of the mask.

# Name that Famous Bear

1. Who was the mascot of the U.S. Forest Fire Prevention Campaign who first appeared in 1944? _____

2. What Teddy Bear came from Darkest Peru and usually wears a blue coat and yellow hat? _____

3. What bear was featured in a series of books illustrated by Maurice Sendak? _____

4. What was the name of the bear of the famous rhyme that had no hair? _____

5. Name the three bears that Goldilocks encountered in the woods. _____

6. What is the group of bears called that includes: Bedtime Bear, Birthday Bear, Cheer Bear, Share Bear, Good Luck Bear, etc.? _____

7. What are the names of the bears that live in JellyStone Park and have their own cartoon? _____

8. What is the name of the bear that appeared in Disney's animated classic, "The Jungle Book"? _____

9. What famous, shy, yellow bear is also a classic Disney character and has a friend named Piglet? _____

# Read, Rock 'n' Roll: Library Idol

## Incentive Summary

The intense popularity of the television reality show, "American Idol" had me racking my brain for ideas on how I could capitalize on it in the media center. Students were constantly coming in asking for books about singers or the American Idol contest, in general. My collection was weak in those areas, so I decided to change that. After purchasing some new books on the subject of rock 'n' roll, singing, bands, and lots of biographies (all listed in this chapter's bibliography), my fellow faculty members and I created a reading theme of it that culminates in a "Library Idol" party.

Students earn an invitation to the Library Idol party by reaching predetermined reading goals. Books should be teacher approved; at our school, we have a requirement that at least one book be a biography or nonfiction book about music or musicians.

As always, you should collaborate as much as possible with teachers on the required amount of reading. It should vary for individual grades, and remember to keep the goal attainable, yet challenging. Students can keep track of their reading with a progress tracker, where they receive initials in the stars on their "gold albums" (for reproducible sample, see page 105). During the month while students are working independently on their reading goals, music is in the air—and in the media center! Suggestions for related activities are included later in this chapter.

At the end of the month, we celebrate our rocking readers by sending them a Rock and Read invitation (for reproducible sample, see page 106). Students are asked to dress like a musician or their favorite American Idol. One of my favorite aspects of these parties is the kids' motivation to see the principal, media specialist, and assistant dressed up completely in theme! After the initial oohing and ahhing over costumes, students are then allowed to take turns cashing in their "golden ticket" to Hollywood by performing on a karaoke machine that we set up (keeping in mind that not all students will want to participate). We allow each guest to vote on their favorite performance, and the winner and runner-up are both given a special prize, which of course includes some music-related books. We also take a group picture as well as individual pictures for the school scrapbook. Each student is given a certificate to commemorate this special event (see page 107 for reproducible sample).However elaborate the set up, students will love this finale to their hard work in reading!

## Food and Decoration Ideas

- Mock performance stage with strobe lights, microphones, karaoke machine, streamers
- Musical decorations bought at most any party supply store or www.orientaltrading.com

- Guitar-shaped cake, possibly titled, "You Rock!" (Some great examples are included on the Web site, www.coolest-birthday-cakes.com/guitar.) Also, many bakeries have template sets that include American Idol copyrighted decorations.

- Musical instruments grouped together as decorations with musical note balloons

- "POPcorn" and of course, soda "POP"

## Bulletin Board/Display

Here is a sample of a display titled, "Read and ROCK! Who will be the next Library Idol?" It creates lots of interest! We also "jazz" up our display using related books and materials, such as miniature instruments, confetti, etc. Get creative!

## Cafeteria Menu

Advertise your incentive program in newsletters, newspapers, and the school Web site. When the whole school participates in an event, students know it must be important. Even the lunchroom can spread a positive atmosphere about the theme. Here are some suggestions:

- American Idol Pie (apple pie)

- Paula Abdul pudding

- POPcorn

- Randy Jackson (dawg' doughnuts)

- Rock 'n' Roll Ravioli

- Ruben Studdard Teddy Bear cookies (teddy grahams)

- Shake, Rattle, and ROLLS!

- Simon Cowell sour tarts

- Singing Sandwiches

- Taylor Hicks Soul Food (BBQ sandwiches)

## Suggested Incentive Activities

- Each week, create a discussion forum about a different genre of music with your students. Introduce them to genres of all kinds, and ask them how music makes them feel, how it makes them want to move, what it makes them think about, etc. Ask them what they think the composer was feeling or thinking when he or she wrote the song. What about the performer?

- With older students, compare and contrast writing lyrics to writing poetry.

- Invite a local folk singer to come in and perform; discuss the relationship between storytelling and folk singing

- Have the music teacher or other musician come in and read during storytime and then do a lesson on how to "READ" notes.

- Work with the music teacher on a cross-curricular class; the music teacher might require a paragraph about a composer using reference tools from the library, and you might require that the students play or perform something they are learning in music together.

- Historical context discussion: Talk with students about the frenzy surrounding American Idol and music in pop culture. If possible, share clips with students, such as the Beatles' appearance on American Bandstand.

- Have students work in groups to change the words to a song of their choice to fit a library-related theme, such as book care, Dewey, etc.

- Have students work in groups to write a rap song about reading.

- Join forces with the P.E. teacher and have students gather in the gym. Provide some historical background about several kinds of music, have them listen to short samples, and then have the P.E. teacher lead them in expressive movement.

- Jokes are a good way to promote what is happening in the media center. It gets kids involved and curious. Morning announcements are an opportune time to reach out to the whole student population. Here are a few that can be read by a student:

  - What did the guitar say to the guitarist? (*Stop picking on me!*)

  - Why did the music teacher get locked out of his classroom? (*He left the keys in the piano.*)

  - What do you get when you drop a piano on an army base? (*A-flat major!*)

  - How many hard rock musicians does it take to change a light bulb? (*Two: One to screw it in and the other to smash the old one on his forehead!*)

## Reference Questions

Have a question of the day on the school intercom, or have a grade-appropriate question displayed during library time and teach students how to find answers. Students can research answers in various ways and turn them in to the media center for prize drawings at the party. Make sure that students document where they found the answer. Use your imagination—this is a great way to portray the importance of the library reference section. Some suggested questions include:

- Who are the names of the performers in the musical group, The Beatles? (*Paul McCartney, John Lennon, George Harrison, and Ringo Starr*)

- What is the musical definition of the term, "rest"? (*A silence*)

- What musical instrument did Beethoven play? (*Piano*)

- Who were the winners of American Idol in the last three years? (*Varies*)

- Who were the first three judges for the TV reality show, American Idol? (*Randy Jackson, Simon Cowell, and Paula Abdul*)

- Name the four main groups of musical instruments. (*Brass, woodwinds, string, percussion*)

- What are the five different types of musical notes? (*Quarter note, half note, whole note, eighth note, and sixteenth note*)

- Between what years do most consider the classical composers came from? (*1750–1820*)

- What is the name of the home of the King of Rock 'n' Roll, Elvis Presley? (*Graceland*) [Question for next day: Where is Graceland located? (*Memphis, Tennessee*)]

## Suggested Reading

- *101 Rock and Roll Jokes and Riddles* by Lisa Eisenberg. Scholastic, 1991.

- *Arthur, It's only Rock 'n' Roll* by Marc Brown. Little, Brown and Company, 2002.

- *Baby Brains Superstar* by Simon James. Candlewick Press, 2005.

- *Bats around the Clock* by Kathi Appelt. HarperCollins, 2000.

- *Boom Chicka Rock* by John Archambault and Suzanne Chitwood. Philomel Books, 2004.

- *Buddy: The Story of Buddy Holly* by Anne Bustard. Simon & Schuster, 2005.

- *Carrie Underwood: American Idol IV* by Kathleen Tracy. Mitchell Lane Publishers, 2005.

- *Dracula Doesn't Rock 'n' Roll* by Debbie Dadey. Scholastic, 2005.

- *Dream Big: American Idol Superstars* series from Mason Crest Publishers.

- *Eelfish, a Rock and Roll King* by Liz Salton. PublishAmerica, 2004.

- *Honky-Tonk Heroes & Hillbilly Angels: The Pioneers of Country and Western Music* by Holly George-Warren. Houghton Mifflin, 2006.

- *Kelly Clarkson* by Jill Wheeler. Checkerboard Books, 2003.

- *Pay the Piper: A Rock 'n' Roll Fairy Tale* by Jane Yolen and Adam Stemple. Starscape, 2007.

- *Pigs Rock* by Melanie Davis Jones. Viking, 2003.

- *Punk Farm* by Jarrett Krosoczka. Knopf, 2005.

- *Punk Farm on Tour* by Jarrett Krosoczka. Knopf, 2007.

- *Rock 'n' Roll Dogs* by David Davis. Pelican Publishing, 2006.

- *Rock a Baby Band* by Kate McMullan and Janie Bynum. Little, Brown and Company, 2003.

- *Scooby-Doo and the Rock 'n' Roll Zombie* by Jesse Leon Mccann. Scholastic, 2007.

- *Shake, Rattle & Roll: The Founders of Rock & Roll* by Holly George-Warren. Houghton Mifflin, 2004.

- *Who Was Elvis Presley?* by Geoff Edgers. Grosset & Dunlap, 2007.

- *Who Were the Beatles?* by Geoff Edgers. Grosset & Dunlap, 2006.

## Related Web Sites

- ***American Idol***, www.americanidol.com

- ***Rock And Roll Hall of Fame***, www.rock-hall.com

- ***Smithsonian Institution***, Electric Guitar invention.smithsonian.org/centerpieces/electricguitar

# Gold Album Progress Tracker

Directions: Every time you reach a reading goal, have a parent or teacher initial a star on your progress tracker. A complete album will earn you an invitation to a Rock "n" Read Party!

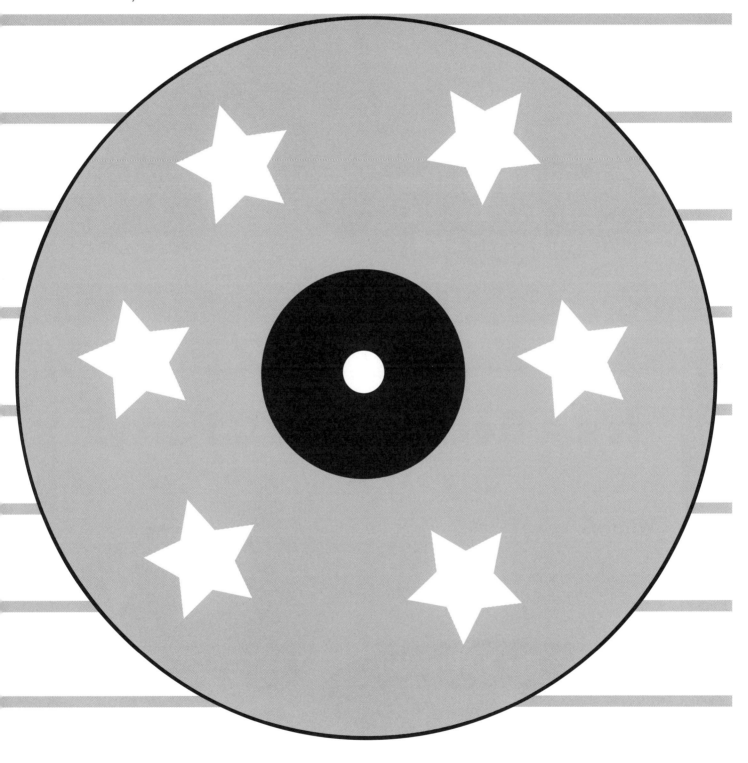

# It's a Rock 'n' READ Party!

Where:

When:

**Dress like a musician or your favorite American Idol!**

# It's a Rock 'n' READ Party!

Where:

When:

**Dress like a musician or your favorite American Idol!**

# YOU CAME . . . YOU READ . . . YOU ROCKED!

_____

**Name**

_____                    _____

**Signature**                                                      **Date**

# YOU CAME . . . YOU READ . . . YOU ROCKED!

_____

**Name**

_____                    _____

**Signature**                                                      **Date**

# We All Scream for Ice Cream!

## Incentive Summary

I scream, you scream, we all scream for ice cream—and we do it outside! Kids and ice cream go hand in hand, and what makes this pairing even better is a beautiful, hot day, and lots of playing and running around with friends. In fact, I can't think of a better theme for the end of school than ice cream! With an outdoor play and ice cream incentive, students gain valuable information—*and* exert some of that extra energy that builds up during the last few months of school.

Set reading goals and have students keep track of their progress by earning scoops on an ice cream reading record (see page 112 for reproducible sample). As always, keep in mind that you must take into account the individual abilities of the students in addition to their grade levels—the reading record and goals can be customized as desired. For this particular incentive, I asked students to read for pleasure at night with a parent or guardian. For every thirty minutes the adult and child read together, they could earn a reading record ice cream scoop. When they turned in their completed records, students received an official invitation to the Outside I Scream for Ice Cream Party! (See page 113 for reproducible sample.)

Students who participate in this incentive at our school are deliciously rewarded at the culminating party. One year, we took a walking field trip to a local park where we had an outside game/play day. Parent volunteers helped make and distribute homemade ice cream while kids made use of the many recreational stations that the adults set up. Ideas include Twister, a bean-bag toss, kickball, badminton, volleyball, Frisbee toss, horseshoes, and more. We handed out certificates upon our return to school (see page 114 for sample).

As you can probably imagine, this incentive is one of the easiest to conduct—and one of the most popular. When you host your ice cream play day, don't forget to take lots of pictures!

## Food and Decoration Ideas

- Ice cream cones or sundaes with all the "fixins" including sprinkles, chocolate syrup, nuts, caramel or butterscotch sauce, whipped cream, and a cherry for the top. Sundaes are a good option for inside parties if the weather ends up stormy.

- Try creating homemade ice cream. We asked for parent volunteers to help with this. Using the graphed surveys from the activities (see activities list in this chapter), we made the most popular ice creams. This option is best when done in correlation with the outside activities party.

## Bulletin Board/Display

Here is a sample of our delicious ice cream bulletin board. Get creative!

## Suggested Incentive Activities

- Have students find recipes on the Internet for homemade ice cream. Find the one with the most ingredients and the one with the least ingredients.

- Have students complete the screamingly delicious webquest on page 115. It is related to one of the more familiar brands of ice cream, Ben & Jerry's.

- Have students work in groups to come up with a new ice cream flavor. They must agree on it, market it, formulate it, and try to persuade others to buy their new flavor. The new flavors can't be introduced until a designated time, and all groups will present on the same day.

- Have students conduct surveys about individuals' favorite ice cream flavors. Separate results by groups; for instance, males/females, adults/children, etc. Have students graph results and display their work.

- Ice Cream Adjectives: Use a thesaurus as a class and come up with as many adjectives as you can that describe ice cream. Then, give students a creative writing assignment to describe their perfect ice cream sundae using as many sensory descriptions as possible.

- Read Shel Silverstein's poem, "Eighteen Flavors."

- Write similes about ice cream such as, "Ice cream is as cool as a cat."

- Using an ice cream die cut, make flash cards into a matching game. Use call numbers on the cone, and the scoops of ice cream can coincide with correct book titles. You can also use this idea with library concepts.

- Discuss the best reference tools to find out about the history of ice cream. Then discuss which reference would be best to find out about Ben and Jerry's ice cream. Why the differences?

- Have the manager from a local ice cream store (Dairy Queen, Baskin Robbins, etc.) come and talk about the ins and outs of the business.

- Using the online library catalog students find and locate one book about ice cream from each section of the media center (easy, fiction, non-fiction).

- There are many educator Web sites that offer clip art and activity sheets on the ice cream theme for every subject area. Check out the Related Web Sites section at the end of this chapter.

- During storytime, begin a story about a hot day and an ice cream truck. Each student should add one sentence to the story. While the story is being told, it should be recorded for playback.

- Older students can make up their own mad lib about the "largest ice cream ever."

- Science teachers can perform experiments about the time it takes for ice cream, or ice cubes, to melt under different conditions.

- Jokes are a good way to promote what is happening in the media center. It gets kids involved and curious. Morning announcements are an opportune time to reach out to the whole student population. Here are a few that can be read by a student:

  - What did the vanilla ice cream say to the chocolate ice cream? *(Have I "melt" you before?)*

  - Where can you learn to make ice cream? *(In sundae school)*

  - What is a geologist's favorite ice cream flavor? *(Rocky road)*

  - How do you make a whale float? *(Get a huge glass, a can of soda, two scoops of ice cream, and a whale.)*

  - Why did the ice cream go out in the rain? *(Because it liked sprinkles!)*

  - What did Ernie say when Bert asked if he wanted some ice cream? *("Sher-Bert!")*

## Reference Questions

Have a question of the day on the school intercom, or have a grade-appropriate question displayed during library time and teach students how to find answers. Students can research answers in various ways and turn them in to the media center for prize drawings at the party. Make sure that students document where they found the answer. Use your imagination—this is a great way to portray the importance of the library reference section. Some suggested questions include:

- What is the freezing point in Fahrenheit? *(32 degrees)*

- When and why was the first ice cream cone developed? *(1904 at the World's Fair. When the ice cream vendor ran out of cups, and folded up his cake to serve the ice cream in, and realized it was a good idea!)*

- Where is the original Ben and Jerry's ice cream plant located? *(Vermont)*

- Which President in 1984 declared July as National Ice Cream Month? *(Ronald Reagan)*

- What are traditionally the 3 flavors in Neapolitan ice cream? *(Chocolate, vanilla, and strawberry)*

## Suggested Reading

Books should always be available around the bulletin board and/or display for student motivation and reference. Students should also be encouraged to venture outside the school library for further material. Here is a good start for this theme:

- *Alphabet Ice Cream: A Fantastic Fun-Filled ABC* (Charlie & Lola) by Sue Heap. Puffin Books, 2007.

- *Eddie's Kitchen and How to Make Good Things to Eat* by Sarah Garland. Frances Lincoln Children's Books, 2008.

- *From Milk to Ice Cream* (Start to Finish) by Stacy Taus-Bolstad. Lerner Publishing Group, 2002.

- *Ghouls Don't Scoop Ice Cream* (The Adventures of the Bailey School Kids, #31) by Debbie Dadey and Marcia Jones. Scholastic Paperbacks, 1998.

- *Ice Cream* by Elisha Cooper. Greenwillow Books, 2002.

- *Ice Cream Dreams* (Spongebob Squarepants) by Nancy Krulik. Simon/Spotlight/Nickelodeon, 2004.

- *Ice Cream Larry* by Daniel Pinkwater. Marshall Cavendish, 2004.

- *Ice Cream: Including Great Moments in Ice Cream History* by Jules Older. Charles-bridge, 2002.

- *Ice Cream: The Full Scoop* by Gail Gibbons. Holiday House, 2008.

- *Isaac the Ice-Cream Truck* by Scott Santoro. Henry Holt & Company, 1999.

- *Milk to Ice Cream* (Welcome Books: How Things are Made) by Inez Snyder. Children's Press, 2003.

- *Mr. Penguin's Ice Cream Adventure* (Little Einstein's Early Reader Level 1) by Susan Ring. Disney Press, 2008.

## Related Web Sites

- ***Baskin Robbins***, www.baskinrobbins.com

- ***Ben and Jerry's***, www.benjerry.com

- ***Edy's***. www.edys.com

- ***Enchanted Learning*** (search "ice cream"), www.enchantedlearning.com

- ***Haagen Dazs***, www.haagen-dazs.com

- ***Homemade ice cream***, www.kidsdomain. com/craft/icecream.html

- ***Ice Cream Alliance***, www.ice-cream.org

- ***Ice cream facts and trivia***, www.makei cecream.com/icecreamtrivia.html

- ***Ice cream history and folklore***, www.food-sci.uoguelph.ca/dairyedu/ichist.html

- ***Ice cream history***, ne.essortment.com/ historyicecrea_ori.htm

- ***Ice cream information***, www.icecream.com

- ***Ice Cream USA***, www.icecreamusa.com

# Ice Cream Reading Record

2 1/2 hours of reading =
2 1/2 hours of partying!

For each 30 minutes of reading, color a
piece of the ice cream cone and have a
parent or teacher sign below.

When your ice cream cone is complete,
turn it in for a party invitation!

 **Parent Signature:**

30 minutes _____

30 minutes _____

30 minutes _____

30 minutes _____

30 minutes _____

# You're Invited to an I Scream, You Scream, We All Scream for ICE CREAM Party!

**Why:** Because You READ!

**When:** To Be Announced
*(You will get a permission slip.)*

**What we will do:** Have fun, play games, and EAT ICE CREAM!

# You're Invited to an I Scream, You Scream, We All Scream for ICE CREAM Party!

**Why:** Because You READ!

**When:** To Be Announced
*(You will get a permission slip.)*

**What we will do:** Have fun, play games, and EAT ICE CREAM!

## I Screamed (and Read) for ICE CREAM!

_____
Name

Insert student's picture here.

_____
Date

## I Screamed (and Read) for ICE CREAM!

_____
Name

Insert student's picture here.

_____
Date